# Angels and Chicken Wings

## BY

## SANDRA LEE

Order this book online at www.trafford.com
or email orders@trafford.com

Most Trafford titles are also available at major online book retailers.

Printed in Victoria, BC, Canada.

ISBN: 978-1-4269-1569-7 (sc)
ISBN: 978-1-4269-1570-3 (hc)

Library of Congress Control Number: 2009935506

*Our mission is to efficiently provide the world's finest, most comprehensive book publishing service, enabling every author to experience success. To find out how to publish your book, your way, and have it available worldwide, visit us online at www.trafford.com*

*Trafford rev. 12/04/09*

 www.trafford.com

**North America & international**
toll-free: 1 888 232 4444 (USA & Canada)
phone: 250 383 6864 ♦ fax: 812 355 4082

# Acknowledgments:

To my grandson Nicholas.
He is my inspiration and my hero. He will always hold a very
special place in my heart.

And also to my loving husband Tim, who continues to give me his
love, patience and support. Without him, my life would not be
complete.

And also to my son Timmy, my daughter Laura and to each of my
four precious grandchildren.
They are the light of my life and they all bring immeasurable
happiness into my world. I love you all!

**John: 3:16**

For God so loved the world, that he gave his
only begotten son, that whosoever believeth
in him should not parish, but have
everlasting life.

# *To You*

Dear Readers,

My hope for this book, to each of you who reads it, is that it reaches into your heart and proves to you that God loves each and every one of us. I want to renew your faith and belief that God is always here for you. I also want to prove to you that God's angels are real and that they do exist. God sends his angels to help us in our everyday lives. I pray that after reading this book, you will believe in them and realize that we are never alone. God is watching over us and his angels are right beside us.

I have written this book because of the inspiration I received from my young grandson. After hearing about his experience, I began to realize that over the years, I too have had many experiences that could have only happened thru the guidance of God. To me, none of these were forgettable and as I began to think about each and every one of them, I realized that they were not meant to be kept to myself. I began to feel compelled and determined to not only tell the world, but to describe my experiences in a way that everyone who reads this book can relate and understand all that I have to say. I wrote it in simple, everyday feelings and language and I hope that it will touch your heart and renew your faith, just as these experiences have done for me.

All the events in this book are real and each one has had a very significant meaning in my life. I changed only the names.

God bless each and every one of you! May you enjoy reading this book and I pray that it changes your feelings and your life forever.

Sandra Lee

# A Gift

SHE WAS THRILLED! The lady sitting across from me could barely contain her enthusiasm and she was hoping that I would agree with her.

The stout, over weight woman was dressed in a silky blouse that draped over her entire upper body. It reminded me of a circus tent that displayed every color in the rainbow. Her thick neck was encircled with layers of colorful beads that hung low on her chest. The beads matched her dangling, gaudy earrings. Her thick, dark, bushy eyebrows were prominent against her milky, white complexion and her whisky voice matched her persona perfectly. When she reached up to push her tousled, short, black hair from the side of her plump, round face, I couldn't help but notice the many sparkling bangles that adorned her arms. The tinkling sound mimicked a giant tin wind chime.

Her long red skirt flowed around her lap, completely covering the over sized chair that she was sitting in. Glancing down at the floor, I noticed that her thick ankles were peeking out from beneath the hem of her skirt, like a shy little puppy hiding under a bush. I couldn't help but think that I was in the presence of a true gypsy. She gave me an uneasy, eerie feeling. I decided right then, that I would regard her as a gypsy lady and not believe that she was a serious, professional woman.

Sitting directly across from her, I was able to observe all her facial expressions as I told her about the unnatural, strange feelings that I have been having. I told her how these feelings came and went without warning and have been steadily increasing in their appearance. I told her that I didn't know how to prevent them from happening or how to make them go away completely. I confessed to her that the feeling not only scared me, but it also terrified me. I asked her if she knew how I could put a stop to these strange occurring episodes.

The gypsy lady listened intently to me and with each and every detail I expressed, her big, dark, brown eyes grew even larger and her wide, plump face seemed to turn an even a whiter shade of white. It was evident that she was getting more and more enthralled as I spoke. She hung on to my every word as if it were her lifeline.

Finally, when I finished speaking, she clasped her hands together with a loud clap and brought them to her upper chest, resting just below her thick neck. The sound from her throat startled me when she let out a loud gasp. She acted astonished as she bubbled over with excitement. I knew right then that what I had just told her, pleased her immensely. She was absolutely thrilled with the detailed description of my recent experiences.

"You have just described something that so many people around the world have spent a lifetime trying to achieve!" she said.

I sat staring at her, unable to believe her words. It was impossible for me to conceive that anyone would want to feel the way I did. I just couldn't believe that anyone would spend a lifetime trying to achieve something so unnatural and eerie feeling. None of this made any sense to me and I asked her to please explain herself.

She lowered her hands and nearly jumped off her chair as she reached out to grab a hold of my hands that were currently engaged in a death grip on the sides of my arm chair. She nearly pulled my arms from their sockets as she tugged me forward and squeezed my hands tightly. In her whisky, rough voice she said: "Don't fight it, go with it. I will teach you to control it!"

Just the sound of her words gave me goose bumps up and down my arms, and as I listened to her continue to explain herself, I couldn't help but feel even more scared than I had previously been. What she had proposed to me didn't sound like anything that I would want to pursue. There was something about what she was saying that just felt wrong to me. Everything she had said completely went against my values and beliefs. I found myself unintentionally discrediting every word that rolled off her lips. Her information and suggestions didn't sound like professional advice and that fact was beginning to worry me.

As I continued to listen to the gypsy lady, each one of her sentences instilled more and more fear within my thoughts. I could hear my heart thumping to the beat of: Not good. Not good. Not good. I didn't like the sound of her explanation or her detailed information and I didn't want to hear anymore of what she had to say. A little voice inside my head told me that it was now time to leave, and I knew I had to listen. I pulled my hands from her tight grip and stood up. A displeased and shocked look replaced the lady's grin as I politely excused myself from her presence and said goodbye.

I walked out the door, closing it behind me. The shiny, silver name plate on the front of the heavy, mahogany door caught my attention and I stopped for a moment. It read: Psychologist. I laughed to myself and snickered out loud: "Yeah, right!" Then turning away quickly, I reasoned to myself: She may have had a degree, but her beliefs and values were running on an opposite track from mine and I wasn't about to stick around to see where her train was headed. I walked towards the elevator and pushed the down button.

I still had a lingering, uneasy feeling after hearing the gypsy lady's words, although, at the same time, I did feel relieved that I had finally gotten a title to give to the unnatural feeling that has been happening to me. I now knew that I wasn't imagining it and I was able to confirm now that I did NOT need a psychologist after all. I had learned that everything that I had been feeling was in fact very real. I felt that I was now making progress in my quest to find the answers to my questions. By talking to the gypsy lady, I had gotten an insight as to what was really happening to me.

So many questions and thoughts were bouncing around in my head as I tried to focus on the most important piece of information that I still needed to find an answer to. The gypsy lady told me that the experiences that I have been having are truly something special, but my instincts told me that there was definitely something not right about them. There was something about them that felt demoniacal to me, and I had to find out if my instincts were correct. I needed to know exactly WHERE these strange feelings had derived from.

As I stood lost in my thoughts waiting for the elevator to stop on the second floor and take me down to the ground level, my thoughts suddenly disappear. I could no longer concentrate and focus. I started to feel almost light headed. I felt like I was drifting away from my mind and my body. I was scared and I started to panic. I wanted to scream out loud: STOP IT! STOP IT! But, I knew it wouldn't help. I could feel that it was starting to happen to me again. And yes, the gypsy lady was right. I didn't know how to control it.

The gypsy lady called it Astro Projection.

Astro Projection is the ability to separate your body into two parts, the physical body from the spiritual body. Your soul basically leaves your human body and becomes energy like in existence.

I WAS UNABLE to make the feeling stop or go away and as I stepped into the elevator, I felt that I was also uncontrollably stepping out of my body. Logically, I knew that my physical body was standing inside the little enclosed space, but I felt that **I** was no longer contained within that human form. As my soul left my human body, I could feel the absence of containment that my body had always provided. I felt that my soul did not have a shape or form. I just seemed to "exist" outside of the confinements of my own human flesh. The cold metal walls and the industrial carpeting temporarily became my skin. The walls of the elevator momentarily were my boundaries and they were holding me in, containing me within their solid formation. I felt huge beyond describable. I had left my physical body and became two individual entities. That physical human body that I called me was standing there and "I" was no longer in it!

The elements of time and space were now gone and I was able to actually feel that they were missing. I felt freed from their restrictions and I could now understand how those elements create a feeling that is naturally unnoticed and unfelt by all solid, human forms of life. The gypsy lady had told me that many people around the world have spent a lifetime trying to achieve this state of existence and I was now able to understand why they would voluntarily want to do this. It does give you the most unimaginable peaceful and freed feeling of existence.

I on the other hand felt very disturbed about the non existent feeling of time, space and substance. I felt both peaceful and freed, but yet at the same time, my instincts were telling me that these feelings were not meant to be felt by human beings on this earth. The lack of those three elements gave me a very intense, eerie feeling and instilled fear within me. I felt that if God had intended humans to experience this, he would have given all of us the ability to do so. We are told in the bible about God's angels, spirits and the heavenly beings that exist without bodies and I am now able to understand how it is all possible. The absence of time, space and substance exists in your soul and it is your soul that lives on forever in heaven. My soul was encompassed with mixed feelings, which I contributed to my lack of acceptance and fear of Astro Projection.

The elevator bell chimed and I was delivered to the ground floor. As my physical body stepped out of the elevator and began walking through the parking lot, I noticed that I currently didn't have the confined feeling that I had felt while I was being held captive within the solid walls of the elevator. In fact, I was feeling freer than I had ever felt before. Outside in the open air with no walls, ceilings or floors to contain me, I was drifting effortlessly above my human form and I couldn't feel an edge to my existence. I was now blending into the particles of the air that surrounded my physical body. My body walked numbly and automatically to my car, but I couldn't feel my human form.

When my body reached my car, I was even more scared of this strange feeling than I had ever been before. The feeling of my spirit being out of my body had lingered longer than it ever has. I was terrified that I would never again be able to return to my human body. I didn't have the control or the know how to make my soul enter back into the person I knew as me.

As my body automatically sat down behind the steering wheel, I felt a new conflict rise within my existence. Anger began to outweigh the feeling of fear in my soul. I had experienced total freedom while being outdoors and the sudden confinement of the vehicle's substance was completely hindering my feeling of freedom. Anger had begun to possess every ounce of my soul. I felt I was forcefully being smashed up against the roof, windows and sides of my car. I had tasted the feeling of freedom without edges or boundaries and its peacefulness overwhelmed me so much that I couldn't resist wanting to be free again. I now didn't like the feeling of containment and I wanted out of the confinement that was again holding me captive. I felt dispersed throughout the entire inside of my car and the conflicting feelings of knowing total freedom mixed with the feeling of being contained against my will, brought my soul to the state of panic. I couldn't think of anything else but the desire of wanting to be freed from the containment that I was currently in.

My body had continued to function normally, doing all the right things, at all the right times, but I didn't have the least bit of control over what it was doing. It was driving the car correctly as if functioning on automatic pilot. It drove home safely, obeying all of the driving rules, knowing exactly how to get where I had intended on going.

For the duration of the thirty minute drive, I struggled with the combined feelings of wanting total freedom and trying to resist giving in to its strong hold on me. When I finally arrived at my driveway, I noticed that I began to have flickering feelings that I was beginning to win my inner battle. For a quick moment I felt myself driving my car. I could feel my hands gripping tightly onto the steering wheel. I could also still feel the entrapped feeling of my soul. The fleeting moments came and went rapidly as I parked my car in the garage and stepped out of the vehicle. Then, just as suddenly as it had left me, my spirit had slipped back into my body. I was now once again my whole person inside my own human form.

For the rest of the afternoon, I felt emotionally drained from the conflicting and terrifying feelings that I had recently experienced. My constant thoughts were continually being haunted by the fact that I knew in my heart that God had not intended humans to achieve this state of existence. My mind and my heart truly feared the source of my experiences.

LATER THAT EVENING, after putting our children to bed, I decided to seek advice from my husband. During the past two months of these occurrences, I had been successful at keeping them hidden from my family and friends. I hadn't told anyone about them (except the psychologist / gypsy lady). I knew that soon it would be happening again and I was hoping that my husband would be able to help me to find an easy answer to my important question. I had hoped that together we could figure out what to do about it before it was too late.

My husband gave me his undivided attention while I explained everything about my experiences and also my recent visit to the psychologist / gypsy lady. I expressed to him my fears, thoughts and all the little details that were involved in these unnatural episodes. He was able to understand my concern for a quick and easy solution. Unfortunately though, he only knew as much about it as I did, which at this point, was very little. However, he did point out to me that my inner feelings were most likely the correct ones. He completely understood my major concern about whether these experiences had derived from something I should fear and if I should try to put a stop too it or, if they were indeed a special gift like the gypsy lady claimed. His advice to me turned out to be the most helpful piece of information that I had received so far. He advised me to pray about it and to tell my concerns to God and ask for his help. We both knew that it wasn't under my control and only God would have the answers that I was seeking.

That night I prayed. And I continued to pray each night, asking God for his help.

Each night lying in bed next to my husband, our backs touching one another, I closed my eyes and silently asked God to help me. I told him how these experiences scared me and that I feared that they may have derived from something evil. I told God that I would accept and be happy with these experiences if he did indeed give them to me as a gift. I also asked him to please take them away from me if it did not come directly from him. In my prayers, I left all my concerns on the lap of God and placed all my faith and trust in him. I asked him to make the decision for me and to somehow tell me what I should do about my current situation. I carried on my conversation with God for three nights. I completely and totally trusted that he would help me.

On the third night, God answered my prayers!

That night as I lay praying, I was jolted out of my prayers by a sudden feeling. It was a warm, strong, pulsating, glowing feeling that began to spread through out my entire body. It originated in my chest and slowly engulfed my entire being. I could feel energy and it felt like that energy was slowly being drained from me. I felt something being gently pulled from every cell in my entire body. I could actually feel the warm flow of energy draining out of me in a pulsating movement. It was a very calming and relaxing feeling and I wasn't the least bit scared at what was happening to me. Fear was the farthest thing from my mind. I knew in my heart that something good was happening.

My curiosity forced me to open my eyes to see if I could visually see what I was feeling. Suddenly, I felt I was no longer alone – excluding my husband who was sleeping soundly next to me. I wanted to see if there was actually something there that was causing this feeling. I could feel that there was and I just had to look at it. I wanted to be able to see where this feeling was coming from. I could no longer resist the temptation to open my eyes and look.

When I opened my eyes, my bedroom was completely dark, except for one area to my left. Our bed was located about four and a half feet from the outside wall. On that same wall to my left, was a medium sized window. The window was completely covered from the top down to the floor with light concealing, lavender drapes. The drapes room darkening material barred even the smallest flicker of any outside light from penetrating thru it and it was in front of those long drapes, that I saw the most truly awesome sight I had ever seen in my life! There was a lit up area and it held a vision that I will never forget!

I saw a bright light in the shape of two very thick bars. The large bars were bent into the exact shape of parentheses. They were approximately four feet apart from each other. Each bar was about three feet in height and about five inches thick. The bars were glowing with a fast, pulsating, and very bright, off white -- almost a light, golden yellow – colored light. I could still feel the pulsating energy flowing from me and it was going directly into the thick, glowing bars. The bars were pulling an energy force from within me with such consistent and steady speed that I felt like an opened faucet dispersing water in steady, even flow.

I couldn't move. I tried to move my body, but it felt like an invisible force was holding me perfectly still. I didn't feel a pressure or any type of constraints holding me still, but I just knew I wasn't supposed to move. Moving my eyes was the only movement I could to make. I tried to lift my arm, but it felt like the air was holding it still. Even my fingers were still and I couldn't move them at all. When I tried to lift one of my legs, it wouldn't move. It felt like a force was keeping them from moving or even flinching. I felt I didn't have a choice but to lie perfectly still and continue to let the energy flow out of me and into the bars. Lying so perfectly still, with the pulsating feeling flowing from me, felt invigorating and yet peaceful. The feeling of energy continued to pulsate and flow out of me and all I felt I wanted to do was smile and stare.

In exactly the center of the two glowing bars stood a figure that was about two and a half feet in height. The figure had the shape of a man. The man was facing me, but his body was turned ever so slightly to his right. He was dressed in a full length, long sleeved, bright, pure white gown that hung down completely covering his feet and I could not see them. The gown was loosely fitted and had many folds in it. The long sleeves were wide and they blended right into his gown. I did not see his hands or maybe I just didn't notice them as his arms were down at his sides. Where his head should have been, I saw a very, very, bright, luminous, white light that completely hid his face. The luminous, bright light had the shape of a circle without defined edges and it shined purer and brighter than any light your mind could imagine. He stood perfectly still and never moved. I could feel that he was staring at me, even though I could not see his face. In my heart I instantly knew who that man was. I whispered in an inaudible sound: "JESUS!"

I continued to stare at the figure before me. I couldn't take my eyes off of it. I didn't want to take me eyes off of it. I was thrilled and excited beyond belief. I was in complete and total awe. Then I thought that I might possibly be dreaming or even hallucinating, so I closed my eyes to test myself. I could still feel the pulsating feeling of the energy being pulled from my body. When I opened my eyes again, the figure and bars were still there -- glowing brighter than ever. The pulsating never stopped. It continued in an even, steady flow. I tried it again, thinking that if the vision went away, it would prove that I indeed was actually dreaming. I closed my eyes and again and when I opened my eyes, everything I saw was still there, just as clear as it ever could be. Nothing had changed.

As the pulsating continued, I felt the urge to wake my husband. I wanted so very much to share this beautiful, breathtaking vision with him. But more so, I wanted to get his confirmation that he saw it too. But still, I couldn't move. I wanted to reach over and shake my husband awake, but again, my arms wouldn't move. I then tried to speak and call to him, but not a sound came out of my mouth when I opened it and tried to speak. My voice was completely gone. I tried again to call to him, but nothing happened when I said his name. I wished I could have shared this vision with my husband, but then my instincts told me that I wasn't supposed too. This vision was meant to be seen by only me.

The site that I saw before me, gave me such a wonderfully, honored feeling that I didn't want to stop looking at it. I no longer had the urge to move or speak and I wanted to lie there -- staring at it forever. I was enjoying this beautiful vision and the feeling of the pulsating, pulling energy flow leaving my body. I felt renewed with each second that had pasted.

I continued to feel the flow of the pulsating energy for about ten minutes in total. For that entire time, Jesus stood within the glowing bars, never leaving my sight. Then as quickly at it appeared, his figure, the bars, and the luminous light, the pulsating energy flow -- it all disappeared! It just stopped. The invisible hold that kept me from moving also went away. I was now able to move my body, but again, I still didn't want too. I just laid there encompassed in complete astonishment. My spirit and my mind felt different than it did just ten minutes ago. A burden had been lifted and my heart felt lighter. I felt cleansed. I was changed.

I closed my eyes and fell into a very peaceful, restful sleep for the remainder of the night.

When I awoke the next morning I couldn't wait to question my husband. I was exploding with excitement when I asked him if he had heard or seen anything throughout the night. His response of course was: "No". He had slept soundly and peacefully all through the night. I couldn't thank him enough for his great advice as I shared with him God's answer to my prayers.

Since that night, twenty one years ago, I have never again felt the feeling of Astro Projection. It went away completely and it has never come back since. God answered my prayers and took away what was evil. I now know that my instincts were correct, and the gypsy lady was wrong! Astro Projection is NOT a special gift from God.

# Our Miracle

MY LIFE HAS been blessed with many miracles from God. Again and again I have received conformation that God answers even the smallest of our prayers. Whenever I think of the many times that I have received help from God, Jesus and his angels, I can't help but become filled with renewed faith and joy. My hope is that you too will open your heart and mind to recall the many blessings you have received also.

The following is just one example of how Jesus answered a simple, three word prayer that escaped from my lips in the moment of terror. As you read this, you will see that it is once again my proof to you that God, Jesus and his angels are always with us and they not only hear every single prayer that we whisper, but they also hear the ones that we scream.

MY HUSBAND'S JOB required that our family transfer to many different states over the course of 26 years. On our fourth move, we transferred to a neighboring state after a nine year stay in our home state of Ohio. We had purchased a home in Rochester Hills, which is a peaceful, suburban town located to the north east of Detroit, Michigan. We had lived in that town for three years and during that time, we experienced the pleasure of making lifetime friendships with our wonderful neighbors. We had also discovered that most of the people in Michigan are friendly and genuinely care about one another. Our neighbors welcomed friendliness easily gave the large town a small town effect, making it a great place to call home.

I truly enjoyed living in Michigan! As each day unfolded, its dramatic climate changes and unpredictable weather continually kept everyone in suspense. Very often, our well prepared plans had to be altered due to constant, sudden weather changing conditions. But that didn't seem to bother me at all. I had lived most of my life in the mid eastern states, which made me very familiar with unpredictable weather. In fact, I feel that it has helped to encouraged me to embrace change and it also taught me how to enjoy the excitement of spontaneity!

Michigan is a beautiful state with magnificent, breathtaking, seasonal changes that constantly filled my eyes, mind and senses with the majestic beauty of nature. God's handy work in this picturesque state showed nature in its full glory with each and every changing season.

In the summer, the lavish, green landscape that surrounded us never seized to amaze my eyes. The bountiful neighborhoods and parks flourished with an abundance of tall trees and deep woods. Mini forests and wide open fields lined the many freeways and roads. The continuous presence of nature's mature, lush landscape not only refreshed and cleansed the air; it also gave you feeling of serenity as you traveled along its pathways.

The autumn season always performed to perfection, a living color wheel of beauty. Red, yellow and orange leaves adorned the many trees with such bold beauty that I found it difficult to stay indoors during the fall season. I always looked forward to the rich fragrance of autumn as it permeated the air when millions of fallen leaves began gathering on the ground.

The winters were picture postcard perfect with blankets of snow that glistened in the afternoon sunlight. The trees bare branches literally sparkle as the sunrays bounce off their frozen limbs and the site of a new falling snow would always rekindle your spirit as it joyously ushered you into the holiday seasons ahead. All of the dramatic changes to the landscape that arrived with each different and changing season encouraged every individual person to accept and welcome nature's beauty with open arms. Michigan truly is a beautiful state that offers a kaleidoscope of ever changing color and weather all around you.

DURING THE DURATION of our three year stay in Michigan, our teenage children developed close friendships and slowly began to transform into young adults. My husband and I couldn't have been any prouder of our son who had completed his high school years and made the decision to attend college. He had chosen a state college in the upper northern part of Michigan and decided that it was time for him to venture out on his own and live on campus. I had been reluctant to agree to these arrangements, but it satisfied me to know that our son would still be within driving distance from our home. Just knowing that we would have the availability to visit him as often as we wished, helped to ease my fears of the first step towards the inevitable "empty nest syndrome" that I was now entering into.

As nature gently pushed us towards the autumn season, it brought with it the day that our son would leave his parents and younger sister behind to begin his new life style. All the preparations for college life had been attended too and I couldn't help but absorb our son's enthusiasm as we planned out his new adventure. I was thrill to be a part of the new frontier that lay ahead of him. The long, eight hour drive to upper state Marquette, Michigan was not only the beginning of our trip; it was also the beginning of independence and freedom for our son.

The early start into our journey began as the morning sunrise slowly started to unfold its self, like a beautiful butterfly bursting out of its cocoon. My car had been loaded with all of his dorm necessities and carefully chosen possessions and we were now ready to proceed into the future.

On the open road, time slipped away quickly as the two of us engaged in conversation and discussed the adventures that lie ahead. Nature seemed to bless us with its approval by giving us a backdrop of perfect weather and gorgeous scenery. The uneventful drive proved to be both relaxing and pleasant for the both of us. We arrived safely to our destination, just short of the estimated arrival time.

Once on campus, I noticed that many parents had taken advantage of the opportunity to get reacquainted with the yester years of college life. We were all welcomed to spend the night in the appropriate gender section of the dorms. I had chosen to accept the invitation and the following day attended a guided tour of the college campus along with all the well prepared events that the college had offered. The wide range of activities that involved parent / student participation helped everyone to adjust to the new surroundings.

Following a noon luncheon that was provided by the school, my son escorted me to the parking lot where we said our temporary goodbyes. It was heartbreaking for me to leave him behind and I couldn't stop the tears that were spilling from my eyes. Hugging him goodbye and having to let go of the young man that now stood before me, instilled a huge hole within my heart. Through teary eyes, I saw standing before me, a man who at one time, many years ago, I had cradled gently in my arms as I rocked him to sleep each night. He was the same baby that had long ago, introduced me to the joys and countless happy moments of motherhood. Our son was now a young adult and I had to let him grow and prosper into the intelligent, thoughtful and kind hearted man that we had raised him to be. I said goodbye with thoughts of visiting him again very soon in the future.

TWO MONTHS HAD past before winter had begun to make an appearance and the rainy days filled with the colorful red, yellow and orange falling leaves were now behind us. Winter was attempting to make its presence known to everyone. The crisp, cold days were beginning to turn the cloud's rain into sparkling white snow that occasionally covered all the deteriorating leaves that gathered on the ground during the fall season. In Michigan, a real hodge-podge of weather is in its full glory in November. One day brings sunshine or rain, while yet another day freezes the landscape, enabling blowing snow to collect and fill all of the grounds little nooks and crannies.

Time was slowly passing by, but it still hadn't helped me to adjust to the idea that my baby has flown from our nest. I missed him terribly and I found that everything reminded me of him. I also discovered what a huge influence he has made on all of our lives. I missed all the shenanigans and constant companionship that he and his best friend consistently contributed to our close knit family. We all missed him dearly and my husband and I were looking forward to visiting our son as soon as possible. That day just couldn't arrive fast enough for me.

It was during the first semester, in early November when we received an invitation from our son's college. The college was hosting an open house and invited all parents to attend. We had decided to take advantage of the opportunity and made plans to drive up north and visit our son. It was during that trip that I once again received help from our heavenly father. He answered my quick, short prayer with a miracle that only he could have provided. It was also a day that reminded me of how strong the power of prayer really is.

THE DAY WE planned to drive to Marquette turned out to be another one of Michigan's beautiful, yet very cold days. The air was crisp from the recent small snow storm that had blown thru our town. The sky was a delicate, light blue and the sun had been working diligently since day break to melt most of the previous light snowfall. Only a few tiny patches of icy snow lay hidden under the lush green shrubs that surrounded our house. All of the town's streets and driveways were washed clean with the water from the melted frozen rain and we were once again able to see the large, green grassy lawns that only yesterday lay beneath a thin blanket of snow. Nestled in the trees, a few of the left over birds who had chosen to remain behind in the soon to be winterized state, sat on the thawing branches while they chirped happily with their songs. It was a perfect day for a nice, long drive.

My husband and I started our long journey with a strong feeling of anticipation to see our son once again. It had been several months since we were together and we both were looking forward to the reunion. We had made plans to celebrate this special occasion by taking our son out for a nice dinner in one of the quaint little restaurants located on the main street in Marquette, after arriving at the college. Our anticipation to see our son steadily grew as we passed each mile marker along the sides of the road.

After several hours of riding in the car, the long drive was proving to be lengthy and tedious, but we were thankful that the traffic on the freeway was very light and free of congestion. We had only a few more hours of open road with sparsely scattered trucks and vehicles that lie between us and our destination. I thought we would never get there and I soon became very impatient while sitting in the passengers seat of my car as my husband drove us north. Our excitement and anticipation grew as we continued to drive mile after mile.

We were about half way into our trip when we had started to notice that the terrain along the sides of the freeway was becoming more and more snow covered. The bright sun seemed to be in conflict with the colder northern air and was unable to melt the blanket of snow that covered the frozen ground that lined the sides of the roadway. The concrete freeway that stretched on for miles ahead of us had been previously cleared by the road crew's plows. The salt that they had sprinkled on the roadway earlier in the day had melted all of the snow and the sun had done its job to dry up most of the leftover water. The roadway was basically dry, allowing driving conditions on the freeway to be perfect. But, as we continued to drive north, we noticed that the outside temperature had been gradually getting colder and colder. The air was winning the battle and no matter how hard the sun worked, it didn't stop the cold air from getting even colder. The airs temperature was dropping at a steady rate. It seemed to get colder and colder by the mile.

Several miles later, we drove up behind an eighteen wheeled semi trailer that was driving in the right hand lane. He was traveling along at the legal posted limit for semis, which was sixty five miles per hour. We continued to leisurely travel behind him for several miles, enjoying the beautiful scenery and cheerful conversation. The semi too, continued on, maintaining his current speed.

After a short while, my husband's patience began to wear thin as we approached a long grade with a slight incline in the road. The driver of the semi shifted gears in an attempt to maintain his speed, but his efforts were fruitless. The extremely heavy weight of his tracker trailer prohibited him from gaining speed. Soon, the large truck was hindering us from driving at the posted legal speed limit for smaller vehicles.

The distraction of the slower moving semi truck brought our conversation to a sudden halt. My husband's attention now needed to be directed towards his driving skills. I diverted my eyes from the glimpses of the landscape that was flickering by on the right side of our car, as I focused my attention on the truck traveling in front of us. At that point, I quickly analyzed the situation and predicted my husband's next move. He was a very skilled driver and I knew that he would attempt to pass the large, slower moving vehicle. I was confident that he would be able pass him safely but, yet at the same time, I felt a really, strong urge to suggest that we should stay where we were and he shouldn't attempt to go around the semi. I didn't feel comfortable with the thought of moving out of the right hand lane. I also was very weary of distracting my husband's attention away from his current thoughts because, I knew that my opinion would most likely aggravate him just a little more. I made a quick decision and decided to keep my thoughts to myself as my eyes quickly scanned the left lane beside us. I saw that no other vehicles were in sight. We were clear to move over into the left lane and drive around the semi to pass him. I remained very quiet.

Our car was about half way in progress up the incline in the road as my husband pushed down on the accelerator to gain enough speed to pass the semi. Our speed was steadily increasing at a fast rate as we slipped past the huge back wheels of the semi truck's trailer. Just as we approached mid way of the semi's trailer, our speed still continuing to increase, the front tires of our car drove onto a patch of "black ice".

Black ice is a thin, almost invisible, layer of ice that is formed when rain or melted snow is on a road surface that is below freezing. When you drive on ice, the driver of the vehicle loses control of the steering wheel. Black ice is feared by all drivers who drive in and thru the states that experience snowfall.

When the tires of our car touched the black ice, it had immediately put us into a tail spin. The front end of our car swerved to the left, while the back end swerved simultaneously to the right. In less than a split second, we had spun around in a complete, three hundred and sixty degree circle. Our car was now facing horizontal on the freeway road and traveling at a fast speed. My husband's hands were moving swiftly, trying to gain control of the spinning steering wheel beneath his fingers. Terrified and looking out over the glossy, red hood of our car, I could see one of the semi's huge, black tires with its shiny, silver lug nuts facing us. The front end of our car was now aimed at the second group of the front tires of the large semi's cab. We were speeding forward, directly towards the shiny lug nuts in the wheel-well of the semi. My husband had taken his foot off the accelerator, but that did not slow down our current speed. The front end of our car smashed into the front wheel-well of the semi, making contact for only a split second. After hitting the spinning wheel of the semi, our car quickly bounced off it, just like a little silver ball in a pinball machine that bounces off the flippers and bumpers.

The swift impact threw our free wheeling vehicle into another three hundred and sixty degree circle. We had spun around again, so fast, that my eyes could only see shutter speed flashes of the scenery as it whirled around us. The force from the spin once again, turned our vehicle back into the direction of the semi. Our car was again pointing horizontal on the freeway, only this time we weren't heading towards the semi's tires. Both my husband and I were so petrified and terrorized that we couldn't utter a sound.

Everything was happening so fast! There wasn't anything that we could do that would prevent us from colliding into the semi again. The force that propelled us had gained even more strength from the second spin of our car. Even a person with the world's most talented driving skills would not have been able to stop our car from spinning out of control. At the moment, everything was working against us. The semi itself was too large and too heavy to allow a faster speed to be gained in such a short time. The incline was also preventing the semi from gaining a faster speed in order to maneuver out of the path of our vehicle. It was inevitable that instant death was only seconds away from both my husband and I.

After spinning around the second time, we were now facing the dead center of the semi's huge trailer. I could see the bottom, dull, silver edge of the long, dirty, tan, steel box that stretched between the large tires of the semi. While looking directly at it, I felt that that steel box was going to be part of our coffin. We were only inches away from it and the sloping front end of our car was aimed to slide directly underneath the mass of cold, strong, hard steel. The bottom edges of our windshield measured just slightly under the bottom edge of the trailer. In less than one split second, we would make contact and more than three fourths of our car would be wedged underneath that tracker trailer due to the strong, propelling force of our rotation. That same force would push us almost to the other side, underneath the trailer. The semi would drag our vehicle sideways until its screeching, hot brakes brought us to a halt. Tiny black, road cinders would be spewing from the last four tires of the trailer.

A vision suddenly flashed before my eyes. I saw the tractor trailer stopped and resting on the side of the freeway, with our shiny red car wedge underneath its trailer. Only the rear end of our car was sticking out. The mangled mess of our car had its drivers side smashed in from the distance that it scraped the concrete as the semi dragged us down the road. I was shocked to find out that this was the way our lives would end. I was horrified and I knew that at this very moment, it was the beginning of the end of our lives. Life was going to be completely over for us. There was no turning back. We couldn't stop it from happening. I felt that there was no possible way that we would survive this! I felt that these were our last moments on earth and our lives were going to end very abruptly.

Swiftly and much faster than the speed of light, my thoughts changed and jumped in a different direction. The thoughts were fleeting through my mind one hundred times faster than a blink of an eye. The scenes from my book of life weren't flashing before my eyes, but my feelings were. I felt terribly sadden by the realization that we weren't going to make it to Marquette to see our son. I could feel his loneliness. All of his sadness and bewilderment washed over me. I could feel his pains of hunger and his questioning fear of why we haven't arrived yet. He would be anxiously waiting for us. He didn't know that we would never be able to have dinner with him again. I felt that he would be waiting and waiting for us and we would never arrive. I could feel his disappointment embracing my body. This was going to hurt him deeply and I wouldn't be able to stop his pain. I saw our daughter and she didn't even know we were dead. As silly as this may sound, the thought flashed in my mind that I wouldn't be the one to call her and tell her what had happened to us. I wouldn't be able to give her the bad news. I wondered who would call her. I felt sorry for her because she would have to hear the devastating news from a stranger. I didn't want us to die like this because I didn't want to hurt my children. I didn't want them to feel any sadness or pain from being left parentless. It wasn't their fault and I felt guilty that we were the ones that would cause them so much pain.

As those thoughts flashed thru my mind, faster than I thought they ever could, I became even more terrified. I felt that we were the ones who would cause our own children to feel the deep depths of sadness. I didn't want to think anymore. I didn't have the time to chase away my worries. No one on earth could help us and my mind ran to the only one who would be able to stop the terror that was in front of us.

I squeezed my eyes shut from the horrifying sight and screamed as loud as I could: **"JESUS HELP US!"**

A second later, my body jerked forward and my head jerked backwards as I felt a strong impact. Our car came to a sudden stop. My body wasn't feeling any pain. I had expected to feel immense pain, but I wasn't hurting at all. I didn't expect to die instantly and without pain. I felt shocked and full of disbelief that I was painless. I wondered how that was possible. I feared that I was really dead and must no longer be able to feel physical pain. Then I sensed that nothing around me was moving and terror griped my heart. The air felt eerily still and silent. I was afraid to open my eyes. I feared what I might see. My body felt frozen in time as I sat perfectly still with my eyes remaining shut, afraid to move. I felt despair and alone. My ears strained to listen for a sound of movement or anything that would indicate that my husband was alive. I refused to accept that there wasn't even the slightest sound coming from his side of the car. I realized that I would rather be dead than live without him. I didn't want to open my eyes and look for fear of what I might see, but I knew I had to look. The last sight my eyes had seen was the bottom edge of the semi's trailer and that image was hauntingly frozen in my mind. I had to open my eyes and replace that horrifying sight.

I forced myself to open my eyes and what I saw before me, was not at all what I had expected. My mind slipped into total confusion as I looked ahead thru the unbroken windshield. I could see the front end of our car up against a small, white, snow covered embankment. The front hood of the car was gleaming in the sunlight and it wasn't mangled or smashed. The interior of the car wasn't damaged either. The dashboard was in perfect condition. Nothing was as I had expected it to be. Our car looked just as it did before we drove onto the black ice. I was confused and couldn't understand how I ended up unscratched and why our car wasn't damaged or mangled. I looked to my right and saw that our vehicle was lying horizontal in a ditch along the side of the freeway. I was confused and didn't know how we got there.

Then a familiar sound jolted me out of my thoughts of confusion. My head turned towards the words that were trembling from my husband's lips. I wanted to cry for joy when I heard his shaky voice say: "Hon, are you alright?"

The sound of his voice was like music to my previous hauntingly, silent ears. I literally could feel my heart explode with happiness when I realized that we were both alive! All the fears and terrifying emotions that I had just felt, melted away with the sound of my husband's voice. My heart slowly calmed as he put his arms around and we rejoiced in a comforting hug.

After we sat silently for several moments, we felt the need to exit our vehicle. The terror that lingered around us seemed to manifest into a thick, invisible, choking smoke. The air inside our vehicle became still and overwhelming as we realized that both of us had just escaped death. We needed to allow the fresh outside air to clear our confused and fuzzy minds. I couldn't stop shaking as the past few moments replayed over and over again in my mind. Miraculously we were both alive and we didn't have a clue as to how it happened.

My husband held tightly onto my hand as we climbed out of the snow covered, steep ditch on the side of the road. He led us to the top of the freeway, where we stood momentarily gazing down at our undamaged vehicle. Neither one of us could believe that not only had we survived, but our vehicle did also. We looked around to see if anyone else had witnessed our accident, but there wasn't anyone in sight.

THE SCREAMING WORDS: "Are you guy's o.k.?" broke our silent thoughts as we looked up towards its direction. We saw a stout, older gentleman huffing and puffing as he ran along the side of the road, in our direction. He was yelling at us, trying to get our attention. His semi trailer was parked on the side of the freeway about four hundred yards from where we were standing. His cab door was left open as he absent mindedly jumped out and abandoned his semi's cab. It was obvious that his concern for us was his main priority. He couldn't seem to reach us fast enough. His blue and red baseball cap almost flew off of his head as he ran towards us, as fast as his short legs could carry him. His heavy flannel shirt waved in the wind from quickening speed.

When he reached us, he was out of breath and he was trembling. We could see that he was clearly as shaken up as we were. All of his blood seemed to have drained downward and his face was as white as a ghost. He couldn't stop shaking and I felt sorry for him. His voice was on a verge of tears as he questioned us over and over again about our safety. He acted like he couldn't believe that we were alive. We assured him that we were both unharmed and then I asked him what had happened. He hung his head low with sorrow and disbelief as he explained his actions. He told us that he saw us spin out of control and then he heard and felt our vehicle hit the front wheel-well of his tire. He then watched us out of his side view mirror as we spun around again. Then thinking quickly, he stepped on his accelerator as hard as he could, but was saddened because the he knew he wouldn't be able to gain enough speed to move the heavy vehicle out of our way. He knew the incline was too large for his load to overcome. He then tried desperately to safely maneuver his semi onto the side of the road without tipping or jack knifing the trailer. He knew that there wasn't enough time to do anything to prevent an accident from happening. He said his heart broke when he looked out his window and saw our vehicle only inches from his trailer. He knew it was over and there was nothing he could do about it.

Then he said, he didn't know what else to do, so he slammed on his breaks, turned his steering wheel and he could hear his wheels sliding on the cinders along side the road. When the semi finally came to a stop, he looked out his window and couldn't see our vehicle anywhere. He thought for sure it was wedged completely under his trailer and hidden from his sight. He shook his head again and said: "I don't know what happened next, but your car was gone. I thought it was under my trailer, but when I jumped out to look, it wasn't there."

Goosebumps covered my entire body as I listened to his words. A lump stuck in my throat when I tried to speak. The man was telling us that only a miracle could have saved us from the instant death that he was witnessing about to happen. He admitted that he didn't know how we could have possibly avoided the collision. He said it was truly impossible that we didn't hit into him. He kept apologizing over and over again for not being able to move his semi truck fast enough to get out of our way. He said he really tried, but he knew he wouldn't be able to stop the inevitable. He watched in horror the vision that played out in his side view mirror.

The gentleman finally, after calming down, realized that he wasn't the one who saved us from death. He stopped shaking and removed his hat from his head. He held it to his chest and slightly grinned. He stood speechless for a few minutes while he absorbed the miracle that he had just witnessed.

Jesus had answered my little three worded prayer that I had screamed in the moment of terror. He had either lifted that several thousand pound semi, moving it out of our way or he moved our vehicle so quickly that neither the gentleman or nor us had been able to see it happen. That is the one and only explanation that the three of us could agree upon. If not for the help of Jesus, today my husband and I would no longer be alive. He gave us a miracle and provided us with the gift of life.

# *Signs*

THE JOURNEY OF life is full of many different types and aspects of signs. We live in a world full of signs. Some of the signs are so prominent that you can't miss them. Others are little ones that seem to be insignificant, even though with a quick glance, they do register within your mind. We acknowledge these types of signs then choose to discard them from memory. Anyway you look at it, whether they are large or small, there are signs telling you what to do, how to do it and what to expect. Without these signs, some people are lost.

All humans have come to depend on some type of "directions" and we are particularly dependent on directions from signs. Whether the signs exist on the sides of the freeways, or the buildings we walk through or simply just a little piece of paper posted on your refrigerator door, we all rely on them. There are signs everywhere. We are a world directed by signs.

"IF" and "HOW" you interpret these signs, is of each person's individual choice. It is a decision made in a split second or sometimes thought out long after you have seen them.

The world is made up of people who consistently read each and every sign, follow all their directions and obey them diligently. There are others who half heartedly read all of the signs then choose to follow only the ones that make sense and that are convenient for them. Still others read almost all the signs but yet, they choose to ignore every one of them.

There are so many signs and variations of signs that you probably couldn't count them, even if you wanted too. Signs exist everywhere and pertain to everything in life. They are around every corner, at every angle, every height and every event. Signs exist literally everywhere.

I highly doubt that there are signs IN heaven, but I positively know that there are signs FROM heaven. These are the signs that are seen, interpreted and felt mostly within your heart. Your mind perceives them, but it's your heart that acknowledges and either accepts them or ignores them. Sometimes they are not very clear and understandable, but they are there none the less. Watching for these signs from heaven and acknowledging them – much like you acknowledge the signs along the roads – can help you in your everyday life. If you BELIEVE in signs from heaven, you will see that they are all around you.

Matthew 2:2 Saying, Where is he that is born King of the Jews? For we have seen his star in the east, and are come to worship him.

Matthew 2:9 When they had heard the king, they departed: and, lo, the star, which they saw in the east, went before them, till it came and stood over where the young child was.

Matthew 2: 10 and when they saw the star, they rejoiced with exceeding great joy.

There are times when you don't realize that you've seen a sign from heaven -- until you are passed it. It's then, that you realize that the sign was there -- only your mind chose not to acknowledge it at the time. We tend to become so preoccupied with emotions and total absorption in what is happening at the moment that we are unable to instantly recognize a sign from God. At these times, the signs can be so subtle that they go unnoticed. Being aware of, looking for and believing in them is the only way to understand and see God's heavenly signs.

It was only after I had walked away, had I realized that God sent me a sign. I wasn't expecting or asking for a sign from him, but he knew I needed one. It wasn't clearly understandable at that moment because my frame of mind was in a totally different place. I was so confused, distressed and heartbroken, that I was unable to recognize the meaning of my experience until it was over. It wasn't until after the fact that I was able to realize that God's sign gave me the comfort and healing that I so desperately needed.

God sends us signs to let us know that he cares and he's always with us. God's signs are his messages to us. He sends them at preciously the right moment that we need them. It is our own individual and personal choice whether or not we want to believe in them, acknowledge them and accept the signs from God. Or, we can reject his signs, just as we reject the man made signs in our everyday life.

The two following chapters describe several significant "signs" that I received from God. These signs comforted me and made me realize that God not only answers our prayers, he also cares enough about us to send us his love even when we don't ask for it. God sent me these signs to show me that even in the time of despair, he is always with us.

# A Sign From Heaven

VALENTINES DAY WAS nearing and so was the end of a major chapter in my life. I was now beginning a new chapter with new events, but one of the main characters was now missing. As I now entered the new section of the book of life, I found the kind of chapter that you are never quite fully prepared to enter. No matter how hard you try to tell yourself that it is all part of life, the ordinary person can never really mentally prepare for death. The death of a loved one crushes all your future hopes and dreams in one short last breath. It can take away your present state of mind and manipulate it into total confusion. It brings forth new and strange feelings of sorrow and heart break that forever etches its self into your mind and heart.

Knowing that the end of my father's life on earth was approaching at a rapid speed, it was difficult for me to find comfort and happiness in my heart. As each day passed by, I watched him fall deeper and deeper into the realms of no return. He tried desperately to fight his battle with cancer, but eventually his strength began to weaken. His battle, unlike the mighty battle he fought in World War 11, had an enemy that was working from within. It was conquering him and taking over the soldier that long ago stood strong and proud. It was waiting in the background to hand him yet another purple heart, the wounded soldiers Medal of Honor.

My father previously hadn't spoken a word in the last few hours and after the last attempt to revive his heart, we knew that the angels were patiently waiting for his arrival. My family members and I stood diligently beside his hospital bed, like the angel soldiers that stand guard at heavens gate. In essence, I felt that we resembled the changing of the guards at an imperial castle – but in our situation, this was going to be heavens imperial castle. We were there beside him as the angels came to usher him into the ever lasting glory of heavenly life.

With each family member standing beside his hospital bed, we took turns saying goodbye and giving him one last kiss. It was my turn and as I wiped away my tears, I leaned down to kiss him goodbye. I whispered to him to ask Jesus for his forgiveness and to welcome him into his heart. I continued to stand there for several more moments, just gazing at him, thinking about how deeply we all loved him. I leaned down again to kiss him one more time and he began to struggle to make an auditable sound. I leaned even closer and listened intently as his whispered gasp said: "Let me go".

After hearing his heart breaking last words, I kissed him one more time and I understood that he was now ready to once again, receive a "purple heart". Only this time, it would be very different because he would be entering thru the gates of heaven to receive his award. I was sure that his purple heart would be made of the finest and purest gold.

In the hours that followed my father's death, I was unable to find peace in my heart. All the happy memories and loving thoughts quickly evaded my mind while I slowly became numb and temporarily out of focus. I seemed to be functioning in a cloak of fog and I thought the fog would never lift. I began to feel that I would now spend the rest of my life living in the mist of empty feelings and unclear endings.

However, the more I thought about "endings", I soon realized that believing in God and heaven meant that there really isn't an ending. We may end our time on earth, but life in heaven goes on forever. That thought alone, comforted me a little. It gave me hope that someday, I will once again reunite with my father.

Having said our last "Good-byes" to my father, my family and I proceeded to make the final arrangements. We made choices, plans and decisions with an unclear mind and a broken heart. Staying close to my mother's side, while offering her as much support and love that we could possible give her, my sister and I helped her make all the difficult decisions. It was a time for our family to unite, to stay close to each other and help one another. Together, we attempted to accomplish all we were instructed to do.

As we continued to spend the following day making all the necessary arrangements together, I couldn't help but notice that I kept hearing a short little phrase, of two small words, over and over again in my mind. It was a constant echo, of which I had no control over. I soon realized that it was a memory of a rough spoken voice saying the words: "You girls" again and again. It felt like a distant memory trying to come alive again. I soon realized that I had heard that phrase all my life, but now, I would never hear it spoken out loud again. It died the day my father did, or so I thought.

I had never paid attention or noticed those two often spoken words, until I was older. It was a phrase my father used all the time. He would often refer to my sister and me as: 'You girls", and while growing up, to me, it just became a natural thing to hear. However, once I was an adult, I became aware of the phrase and realized that to him it meant something special. I realized that for him, it seemed to be much easier to group the two of us together rather than saying our individual names. To me, it subconsciously sounded good. It always made me feel included. It represented that my sister and I were always in his thoughts together – both at the same time. It also showed me that he thought of us as two people who would always be "together" in his mind. I realized that to him, it really did mean: the BOTH of us, and this simple phrase showed that our father didn't want us to feel that either of us would be left out or forgotten. In my father's mind, it was a quicker and much simpler way of including both of us in his thoughts, at the same time.

Now I had wondered if he would be looking down on us, watching our every move and smiling, knowing that his "girls" were together, helping our mother cope with her life as it crumbled and fell apart around her. My father's "girls" had to stay united and be strong while we supported our mother. This was a time in our lives that we needed each other. Together, we needed to be our father's "girls".

THERE WERE so many little details that needed attended too. The first item on our list was to order the flowers that would surround the casket. We had decided to purchase them from the flower shop within the local grocery store where my father had worked part time as a grocery bagger after his retirement. His job not only instilled a sense of purpose and self worth, but a feeling that he could still provide for his wife. He was the man of the household and he was still able to bring home a paycheck.

It was very difficult for us to walk thru the entrance of that particular store. A rush of emotions swept through our hearts and a strange, new, empty feeling washed completely over us as we entered. We had to fight the instinct for our eyes to scan the front of the store, looking for my father to be hard at work. We had to erase from our minds, the thought that he would be standing there smiling at us and eager to introduce us to the current cashier or customer. Being the outgoing person that he was, my father really enjoyed his job.

Bagging groceries and loading them into the customers trunk was just one of the many little duties that his job consisted of. Often times, he made it his own personal priority to bring smiles and giggles to the bored, cranky and tired children that passed through his check out lane. Each and every child always left with a smile. During the slow check out times, he would walk through the parking lot, retrieving all the abandoned grocery carts and return them to the cart corral at the front of the store. He not only considered this just part of his job – it was also an opportunity for him to enjoy the fresh air and sunshine while escaping the noise and commotion of the busy store front area.

The next and last item on our "to do" list, was to visit one more local store. We had a mission to accomplish and it was slowly nearing completion. We were grateful that the ladies auxiliary club from my parents little town, had offered to host a family dinner following my father's burial. Supplying the beverages and paper products became our responsibility for this event. By purchasing these, we would complete the last item on our list.

At the beginning of the day, I had elected myself as chauffer of my mother's car and I was relieved that this would be our last stop. Physically and mentally exhausted, I chose the first available parking space in the crowded parking lot. It was near the end of the parking area. After parking my mothers light blue, Chevy Impala, we solemnly walked together into the store. As we entered the store, we had noticed the many pretty, colorful Valentine decorations that hung from the ceiling above. The store had literally gone overboard with decorations! Big red and pink hearts were everywhere. There were hundreds of them and they were gaily intertwined with red and pink streamers. We were aware that Valentines Day was only two days away; however, we were too saddened too voice our acknowledgement of its existence and the festive appearance that the decorations created. Instead, we were like unfeeling robots, gathering anything we thought that would be needed as we filled the store cart to capacity. After paying for our purchases, we walked together in silence through the crowded parking lot.

My mind was clearly pre-occupied and upon arriving at our parked car, I had neglected to unlock the car doors. My mother patiently stood at the front passenger's door, while my sister and I began to unload the cart in silence. While putting the bags into the trunk, my thoughts flashed back to the grocery store. I pictured my father hard at work, smiling and making small talk with the customers as he was loading bags into a their trunk. I began to think how I was presently doing something that he had done a million times before. I felt that it would be in my fathers honor if I walked the cart back to the store instead of leaving it abandoned next to our car. I knew he would have appreciated that.

Placing the last bag into the already full trunk, I numbly turned around to grab the empty cart. As I began to place my hands on the cart, I raised my head and there, on the opposite end of the cart, stood a short, older gentleman – about 75 years of age. His hands were placed on the opposite end of my cart. They were rough, weathered hands, kind of thick, with plump fingers. He stood about five feet four inches in height and he had a familiar looking face, although I couldn't instantly match it with anyone I knew. His face showed his age and it too had a weathered look - as if he had spent a lot of time in the sun. His skin was tanned and creased with wrinkles. He had mostly gray hair that hid his underlying light brown diminishing hairs. His eyes were a light, crystal blue that were squinting from the rays of the sun. His clothing resembled that of a man who had been working. He wore washed out, baggy, gray khaki pants and a heavy, large gray and blue flannel long sleeve shirt that covered a faded blue tee-shirt. His eyes were full of mixed emotions, yet each emotion seemed to be clearly defined. They were glistening with total inner peacefulness, happiness and anxious anticipation, all of which seemed to be bundled into the light pools of blue. Together, his facial expression and his eyes showed that he wasn't a man of many words, but I could feel that he was anticipating the chance to say something to me.

As a smile came across his face, his facial expression conveyed over-whelming kindness, genuine peacefulness and concern. His thoughts and concern seemed to come from deep within his heart. It conveyed to me that, somehow, he knew what I was feeling and he understood why I looked so distressed. It was a puzzling feeling and I wondered how he could possibly know. It was just impossible for this stranger to know how I felt, but yet, I felt that he completely understood my sadness and I could sense that he felt very sympathetic towards me. But, at the same time, I also felt that he wanted to share HIS thoughts with me. Why? I didn't know, but I felt that he did.

The sound of his voice chased away my thoughts and I focused my attention on the kind gentleman. His voice was very peaceful and soft. It had a calm sincerity about it. I could sense that he really wanted to talk to me and perhaps tell me something that he felt was very important. I could feel that for some reason, he wanted to make this moment last as long as he could. He definitely didn't seem to be in a hurry.

"I'll take that cart young lady" he said as I blankly stared at the kind gentleman. I was grateful that I could now quickly be on my way and I would not have to walk the cart all the way back to the store. I smiled and thanked him, expecting him to turn away and walk towards the store front. But, he didn't move. He just continued to stand there, gazing at me with an explosive happy smile on his face. His weathered hands were still clutching the cart and he was now gazing at me as if I was the most beautiful person he had ever seen. I started to get an uncomfortable feeling, and felt that I was being rude and I should be saying something to him, but I didn't know what to say. I forced myself to smile again and then quickly turned my head away. I didn't want to stand there and carry on a conversation. I was not in the mood to be exceptionally talkative. Again, I expected him to turn away, pushing the cart in front of him.

But, the kind gentleman just stood there – silently. He continued to gaze at me with a smile on his face. Then he spoke again as his eyes glanced back and forth from me to my sister. "Has anyone wished you girls a Happy Easter yet"? "No" I replied, as I thought to myself – EASTER? Why would he mention Easter? Valentines Day is just a few days away and the thoughts of Easter haven't even entered my mind. It sounded strange for him to bring up a holiday that was so far away. Didn't he know it was soon to be Valentines Day? Surely, no one is thinking of Easter yet.

We continued to stand in silence. The trunk of the car was still open. His hands were still clutching the opposite end of the cart. The smile never left his face. I felt that he was going to stand there forever. He kept glancing back and forth from me to my sister as if he really enjoyed looking at us. We were both staring at him and I began to feel the need that I should say something again to the kind gentleman. "Well, Happy Valentines Day" was all I could think of to say. I was still unable to conceive the thoughts of future holidays and I completely ignored his Easter greeting. I had expected that he would now respond with acknowledgement of the current event. But instead, with his same soft, peaceful voice he replied: "Happy

Easter girls!" Immediately and mechanically, my sister and I both replied with: "Happy Valentines day". We had both ignored his Easter greeting.

The kind gentleman's face quickly showed a hurtful look and I could see disappointment in his light blue eyes. He seemed to be dissatisfied with our response, although he made no attempt to walk away. I suddenly felt as if we had offended him. His facial expression became so sad that I felt that we had not only offended him, but that we had also hurt his feelings. As I stared into his eyes, I could see that their expression was clearly trying to say something. They seemed to be sadly saying to us: You're not really listening to me and why don't you understand? It was then that I realized that he was stubbornly choosing to ignore Valentines Day. The long pauses between conversations began to feel slightly uncomfortable to me, but it was also obvious to me that he enjoying our conversation, even as little as it was. Then suddenly, I realized that he was genuinely happy about the opportunity to talk to us and that he would continue standing there until we acknowledged his point of thought. He wanted us to wish him a happy EASTER -- and not a happy Valentines Day!

As these thoughts slowly began to register in my mind, the sweet, peaceful smile returned to his face and he once again repeated himself: "Happy Easter girls!" Hearing those words again, I couldn't help but return a half hearted smile to the kind gentleman.

Once again he spoke, but this time there was real importance and excitement in his voice as he said: "I want to be the first one to wish you girls a Happy Easter!" There was silence for a short second or two before my sister and I both simultaneously wished him a "Happy Easter". Our immediate response seemed to greatly satisfy him and he showed contentment as he smiled back at us ever so lovingly.

With this satisfaction, the kind gentleman slowly turned his sparkling eyes upwards towards our mother, who was still standing silently and patiently at the unlocked car door. Sadness and despair had overwhelmed her face. Her broken heart overtook her thoughts and she showed no previous awareness of the kind gentleman. He was now gazing at her as if she had all along been part of our conversation. The kind gentleman smiled ever so sweetly at her and joyfully said: "You too Grandma - Happy Easter"! The sound of his raised voice jolted her back into reality and she instantly responded with a sad, soft voice and wished him a Happy Easter too. Hearing my mother's saddened voice brought tears to my heart and made me realize that even though she said the words, her future holidays would not be happy ones. My heart cried for her.

As my sister and I turned our heads back towards the gentleman, we saw that he was once again gazing at us. His smile showed great contentment and inner happiness. He looked proud and pleased that he had gotten his point across to us and we had acknowledged his excitement about the up-coming Easter holiday. His clear blue eyes were twinkling, not from the sun, but from real inner happiness. He was still clutching onto the cart and he once again said with a joyous voice: "Happy Easter Girls!" With that, he stood for only another moment, and then he turned and began to push the cart towards the store front. I watched him walk away for only a second, before I looked away.

As if still in my fog and unable to analyze this strange conversation, I mechanically slammed the trunk closed and proceeded to walk to the driver's side of the car. After unlocking the doors, my mother, sister and I slid into our seats and it was exactly at that precise moment that my sister and I realized who that gentleman really was!

Tears began to stream down my face as I turned my head towards my sister sitting in the back seat. She too had a flood of tears coming from her eyes. At the same instant we both exclaimed aloud: "That was Dad!" My eyes lifted up slightly to look out the rear window of the car in hopes to get a last glance at the kind gentleman - but he was gone. He was no where in sight!

Smiling and looking at my sister while we both choked back tears of happiness, I whispered: "That was daddy". And she answered: "I know".

Hebrews 13: 1 – 2

Let brotherly love continue. Do not forget to entertain strangers, for by so doing some have unwittingly entertained angels.

# Analysing The Sign

LIKE SO MANY signs that exist in our world today, so do the signs from heaven. These signs are sent to us, not only to encourage, comfort or bring peace to our hearts, they are also sent to let us know that God cares. God orchestrates these signs so precisely and with such significant detail that it's impossible to ignore. Other times, we receive signs that are so subtle; they feel like little nudges sent from heaven.

My unforgettable experience has changed my thinking to a different perspective of the existence of God's angels. Having thought this over for many years, I have come to realize that there is proof that God's angels do exist. They exist here on earth and they are all around us. I now know that the kind gentleman wasn't an ordinary person. He was an angel sent from God. He was used to deliver a message to us. The message told us that our father was indeed in God's care and that thought brought smiles to our hearts and peace to our minds.

Both my sister and I had gone past the sign before we were able to analyze or process our experience. However, we did see it, and we did recognize that it was a sign from God and that God had wanted us to understand it - but only after the fact. We weren't meant to understand until the angel had left.

There is no doubt that this angel was sent from God, and he had a mission. Looking at the details of this experience, one must realize that the details were too perfect to be anything but a message sent from God. Every detail was clear and precise and in a short span of time, he accomplished many things.

The first detail was location. The entire experience took place in a parking lot outside of a store. It was a store much like the store that my father had worked at. Returning carts to their corral was part of his job and I was mentally intending to return the cart to where it belonged. The gentleman was retrieving the cart from me – the same as my father would have done at his job. The stores many colorful decorations were important also. It was abundantly decorated to remind patrons to acknowledge and observe the Valentines Day celebration. The store was chosen to prove that Valentines Day is not a Christian holiday and therefore, not recognized by the kind gentleman. He repeatedly expressed to us that this kind of celebration did not exit to him.

The third detail was the angel himself that delivered the message. (Recalling that he reminded me of someone) God chose his body build, looks and even his clothing to resemble that of my father. Even his hands were tanned and weathered - short and plump. His eyes were blue. His hair was white. His clothing was all too familiar. The gentleman was close to, if not the same age, as my father.

God had orchestrated every tiny, specific detail. All the details about this gentleman resembled my father, but yet, because it wasn't him physically standing there in his earthly body, and because our minds were pre-occupied, we were unable to recognize the resemblance immediately.

The conversation between us had the most important meaning. He didn't say long, wordy sentences. In fact, they were short and brief with no detail. But, they were extremely powerful and effective. Their impact was strong and precise.

When he said: "Has anyone wished you girls a happy Easter yet?" it represented several points that he wanted us to realize. Most importantly, with that one sentence, he immediately brought God and Jesus to the forefront of our thoughts and conversation. With that single sentence, he was reminding us that the current event of Valentines Day is a man made celebration. It does not have anything to do with God, Jesus or Christian beliefs. The gentleman was telling us that Easter is one of God's important celebrations and that we should have been in anticipation of the Easter holiday instead of a man made holiday. He was insistent upon us realizing that by consistently and completely ignoring MY recognition of Valentines Day. He repeated himself until I verbally acknowledge Easter as the most important upcoming and joyous holiday. He wanted us to join with him in his excited anticipation to celebrate Easter. By wishing him a Happy Easter, I showed him that I was agreeing to always remember to put the celebration of God before a man made holiday.

After delivering God's message to us, he moved on to deliver his message – another part of his short sentence. He used the phrase: "you girls" again and again. He wanted us to indirectly know who he REALLY was. We had been so distracted with our own grief, that we were mentally unaware and unable to notice his constant use of that particular phrase. He was clearing telling us who he was. The excitement in his voice showed us how privileged he had felt to be able to deliver God's message and how happy he truly was. God allowed his newest angel the honor of replacing the grief in our hearts with happiness and reassurance. The over whelming grief that I was feeling, was quickly replaced with tears of joy when I realized that it WAS our father and that God had allowed him to talk to "his girls" -- one last time!

Another point to recognize is the fact that this gentleman acknowledged our mother as a grandmother. This indication showed that he knew – without a doubt – that she had grandchildren. That phrase was a direct and positive way to verbalize his identity. Although, some would argue that the chances of most older women being a grandmother is great, his direct and assured attitude, doubtlessness and the unquestioning, confident expression on his face showed that he knew that she was indeed a grandmother. It was also clear that, even though he was supposed to be a stranger, he completely understood her confused and distraught state of mind. He knew that she would not be able to recognize him for who he really was and he acknowledged her only after he established his first priority – to remind us that God should be the center of all our celebrations.

One last thought about this that has stayed with me through the years, is that this one particular experience had to have had an even greater purpose. I feel that this book is that purpose. It wasn't until I started writing this, had I realized just how much God and his angels have helped me cope with life.

God's angels are among us. This experience is my proof!

# Angel Feathers In My Soul

Little bits and pieces were falling from my heart,
I could feel it crumbling – as it fell apart.
The little chunks all red and dried,
Filled my chest, deep inside.

My eyes were blurry, I could not see,
I looked thru water, at my life around me.
My body shook and quivered my skin,
I felt an aching, from deep within.

My mind was trapped within a globe,
A thick fog of memories, it did hold.
With thick glass walls, its shape was round,
My release was impossible, no edges could be found.

I felt a subtle flutter within the surrounding air,
And realized that suddenly, someone was there.

Although, nothing had changed for my eyes to see,
I felt a golden blanket gently engulfing me.
I could feel its warmth caressing my soul,
Its comfort delivering and invisible glow.

I saw white little feathers as light as snow,
Each one held my shattered hearts pieces in tow.
They were floating and cradling each little part,
And I felt them gently fixing my broken heart.

The feathers gently cradled each little bit,
They placed them exactly where they should fit.

My heart began to shimmer, as it filled with peace,
I began to feel my pain suddenly release.

God sent an angel from above,
And He delivered to me all His love.
His comfort I felt when I needed Him most,
God the Father, the Son and the Holy Ghost!

Sandra Lee

# Sounds From Heaven

A LATE MAY breeze drifted thru the opened bedroom window as I laid watching the sheer, white ruffled curtains dance gracefully in the gentle breeze. The full moon's light streamed thru my window and cast a silvery haze as if it were shining a spot light on a theaters stage. I could almost feel that the light was without substance as it shimmered throughout the room. My bed sheets had an almost luminous glow as the moon beams reflected off their cool, white softness. I felt that I was snuggling into a soft cloud of fluffy, white cotton balls trimmed in lavender as I gently pulled the covers up around me, tucking myself into a nest of calming peacefulness. The crisp, fresh air was drizzled with a light fragrance from the blooming jasmine vines that grew beneath my window, and their sweet, light scent filled the air. I closed my eyes as I slowly inhaled the delicate waves of the fragrant jasmine. The peacefulness was over whelming and my mind began to drift.

I couldn't help but smile as I recalled the memory of the previous Saturday. It was a day that I will always cherish in my thoughts and my heart because; my daughter had made it so very special. She had spent countless hours planning, preparing, cooking and decorating and she had set the stage to showcase a birthday celebration that was nothing but perfection. The entire downstairs of her home looked as if she had waved a magic wand and turned it into a party hall. Every tiny detail was thought out and the outcome couldn't have been more festive or enjoyable!

I remember stepping inside the front door and how my eyes were immediately drawn to the eighteen foot wall to my left. It was covered with a huge rainbow of twinkling lights. There were purple streamers that dangled down from the high ceiling in the foyer. Random lengths of curly ribbons were tied to silver and purple balloons that floated effortlessly above the heads of mingling family and friends. Off to the right, the vaulted living room ceiling was completely hidden by yards and yards of delicate, lavender Tule. It was stretched from one far end of the room to the other. Nestled inside the Tule, were hundreds of silver and purple helium filled balloons just waiting to be released onto the heads of everyone below.

The D.J. sat tucked away and out of sight in the loft that overlooked the festivities below. His music drifted in the air like a cool summer breeze that wrapped each guest in a blanket of festivities. In the far corner of one room, a character artist busied himself with paper and drawing tools. Guests had gathered around him waiting in anticipation to see their most prominent feature sketched into a comical character. In the over sized, kitchen/dinning area, the table was filled to capacity with a large assortment of everyone's favorite munchies. In the center of the table, a huge, scrumptious looking combo cake displayed a happy birthday message to me and my son-in-law. Having been born in the same month, we were able to share our special occasion together. We had exactly a ten year difference in age and this one particular year, we had both reached a milestone.

Adjacent to the table, the kitchen counters were filled with a banquet of varied mouth waters foods. The smell of fresh baked, home-made lasagna permeated the air. Little children scampered about, pulling silver and purple balloons by their long ribbons as they wiggled around and between the forests of adult legs. Even the back patio gave way to the festivities. Every flower box and planter was overflowing with freshly planted blooms that burst with color. Everything looked beautiful!

As I thought about this past joyful celebration, I began to recall the many other birthdays and holidays that my family has celebrated together over the years. We had had so many good times together. There were so many happy memories. I began to flip though the photo album stored deep within my mind. I could see each individual person, smiling and laughing. I saw each family member enjoying a wonderful time.

While I laid there mentally flipping through my minds photo album, I couldn't help but feel the wave of sadness that had slowly begun to creep into my thoughts. There was an empty sad feeling that was growing in my heart. I tried to dismiss the feeling, but I soon realized why I began to feel that way and where it was coming from. It evolved from the thought that I can no longer add more of my parent's photos to my minds album. Several years ago, my family unit had been broken, along with part of my heart, when my parents passed away. I realized that a link was missing and I started to yearn for the completed family unit that I knew I would never again have.

The thought that I would never again hear their voices or feel their touch became so overwhelming that I began to cry. I knew that they were out of my grasp; and they were permanently out of my life. I felt that my heart will always and forever have a piece missing.

I opened my teary eyes and I could still see the soft glow from the moon beams lighting up my bedroom. But, my ears didn't hear the silence that filled the room. Instead, my ears were listening to a faded memory. The sound seemed so far away and faint. I concentrated hard and tried to focus on the verbal part of my minds photo album. I tried to remember the sound of my parent's voices singing happy birthday to me, as they have always done in the past. Every year of my adult life, without fail, my parents called me and they would sing happy birthday to me as my eyes filled with tears and my heart would overflow with happiness. Their singing phone call had become our little tradition and I had never thought that it would come to an end. Now, I longed to hear their voices again. I wanted to hear them sing happy birthday to me – especially now.  It's my fiftieth birthday and I wished I could hear their sweet, singing voices – just one more time.

I wiped away my tears and began to wonder if wishes really can come true. In my heart, I knew where I could find the answer to that question.  I began to pray.

I asked God to please let me know if my parents are thinking of me. I asked him to give me a sign. I couldn't feel that they were near and I needed reassurance that they still loved me.  I wanted so desperately to know that they still cared about me.  I wondered if they knew it was my birthday.  Did they remember that tomorrow is a special day for me?  Will they sing the happy birthday song to me – even if I can't hear it?  I said I was sorry that I never expressed to them just how much it meant to me to hear them sing that song. I wished I had told them.

With those thoughts and prayers, I drifted off to sleep.

Matthew 21:22

And all things, whatsoever ye shall ask in prayer, believing, ye shall receive.

# May 27, 2005

THE NEXT MORNING I awoke. My birthday had arrived. It was exactly 50 years ago that I was born! I had secretly wished for this particular day to be far from ordinary, but it began just like every other day. I got dressed and went to work as usual.

When I had arrived at the office, all my co-workers had wished me a happy birthday and I found myself very pleased that they had all remembered. I was also happy to hear that they had planned to take me out for a "birthday lunch".

The morning had gone by quickly and lunch time had soon arrived and I was given the privilege of choosing any restaurant that I desired. Without needing much thought, I quickly choose a local seafood restaurant only a few miles from our office. It was a causal restaurant that was famous for serving fresh and delicious crab legs and various seafood delicacies. Its décor made you feel that you were on one of the many wharfs that were sprinkled along the California coast line. It was rustic, with wooden tables and flooring made of huge planks of weathered looking wood. Ocean memorabilia adorned the walls and thick heavy ropes were tied around posts as if they were waiting to be attached to the incoming ships hulls. The wooden tables were randomly spaced apart from each other, giving you the feeling of being in a large ship's galley. The center of each wooden table had a large hole cut into it. Into the hole was placed a tin bucket that held a roll of brown paper towels, making it convenient to wipe your hands after indulging in the most delicious, tender, butter dripping crab legs. This was by far, one of my most favorite restaurants!

Upon arriving at the restaurant, I was pre-occupied and I had completely forgotten that the owner of this famous chain of restaurants definitely had a sense of humor, even though it was obvious from the moment you walked in. The entrance was made up to look like a little store where they sold logo tee-shirts and souvenir's relating to their restaurant. A hostess greeted us with a smile and each of the waiters and waitress's wore a tee shirt with comical sayings imprinted on them, all referring to crabs, fish and varied sea life.

Once our small group of six people had arrived, we were seated at which seemed to be, the center of the dinning room. We soon became involved in discussing the menu choices and the current affairs at our office. We hadn't paid any attention to the other guest's that were arriving and filling the restaurant to capacity. There was no way for us to have known that a very special group of people had been seated at a long, extended table, next to ours.

It wasn't quite an hour after our arrival that a large commotion within the restaurant had erupted. I had been so involved with our conversation that I had forgotten that it was my birthday and I hadn't noticed that one of my friends had gotten up from our table and informed the restaurant staff that it was my 50th birthday and we were celebrating with an office luncheon.

At the sound of the commotion, our conversation stopped and I realized that our waitress was now standing behind my chair. She was clapping her hands together and was speaking in a loud voice that demanded everyone's attention. She announced to everyone within earshot that it was my 50th birthday. Then she instructed me to stand up. As I stood up, with complete embarrassment, I could feel everyone's eyes staring at me. I could hear everyone's little snickering giggles. I could feel my cheeks flush and I know I must have turned at least ten different shades of red!

After announcing to everyone that it was my birthday, our waitress requested everyone's co-operation to help me celebrate my birthday. THEN – as if that wasn't embarrassing enough – she placed a hat on my head. And it wasn't just an ordinary hat. It was the craziest looking hat I'd have ever seen. It was made up of long, huge, wild looking, fluorescent pink feathers! While my face blushed with a bright pink color – matching perfectly with the fluorescent pink feathers – our waitress began giving ME instructions! I was told that I must walk the perimeter of the restaurant while smiling and waving too all the guests as they sang the happy birthday song. I was also told that if I stopped waving to them – at any point – they would restart the song and I would have to restart my walk from the beginning. She informed me that this would continue until I had completed a full circle around the restaurant without stopping.

Having had enough embarrassment to last a life time, I quickly began my walk. I waved and smiled at each laughing restaurant guest as they sang happy birthday to me. I didn't dare to hesitate for one second and I was sure that I had completed my tour of the restaurant in what had to be record time.

Arriving back at my chair, still clearly full of embarrassment, I removed my "beautiful", fluorescent pink hat and I sat down as quick as possible. My co-workers and I had thought that all the attention drawn to me had ended and we began laughing and talking about my recent five minutes of fame. Little did we know that there was still more to come!

Still trying to hide my embarrassment, I kept my head low and my eyes averted from the surrounding environment as I listened to the conversation and laughter of my friends. I had hoped that soon, everyone would forget about the embarrassing moment that had just happened. I had my doubts that I would ever forget, but I silently wished my friends would eventually not remember my flushed pink face and fluorescent pink feathers on my head!

Suddenly, our table became very quiet. Everyone stopped talking at once. Noticing this, I looked up from my plate of cold French fries – which I had been fiddling with for the past few minutes. As I looked across the table, I saw a young girl, about fifteen years of age, with short blonde hair. She was standing directly across from me at the other end of the table. She gave me a sweet, adoring smile. She was dressed in a black tee shirt with the words: "Girls Traveling Choir" printed across her chest in bold white letters. Within moments, another girl appeared next to her. She was dressed in the same kind of black tee shirt. Next to her appeared another young girl. And another. And another. They kept appearing until our whole table was completely encircled with the young, teenaged girls, all dressed in black tee shirts. Noticing this, the entire restaurant became silent. It was as if God had suddenly turned down the volume.

Surprised and bewildered, my friends and I didn't utter a word. We sat in complete silence, staring at the girls, as we wondered what was going to happen next. We had no idea that sitting next to us at the long, extended table, was a group of about twenty young girls who had belonged to a traveling choir. They were there with their instructor, having lunch, just as we were.

As I focused my eyes on the first girl that had appeared at our table, she continued to smile at me as she began to hum a note. Instantaneously, each and every girl joined her in perfect harmony. They began to sing happy birthday to me!

Their voices sounded like angels singing, so soft and delicate. It was the most beautiful blend of heavenly voices and harmony that I had ever heard. I could feel love projecting from that one girl and it filled my entire being with joy and amazement. In her eyes, I could see a genuine inner knowledge that she knew that she was doing something really special. Her eyes were filled with understanding, delight and pride. I looked around and saw that even my friends were moved and touched by this unusual display of attention. In my heart, I myself felt that I was hearing God's choir of angels singing, and they were singing just to me!

My eyes closed for a moment as they filled up with tears of real happiness. I had realized that God had heard me and that he was answering my prayer from the night before! God was working through the hearts and voices of these young girls and by doing this, he was allowing my parents to sing happy birthday to me – just one more time! He listened to my prayers and he orchestrated this choir of young girls to be at this particular restaurant at the same time that I was. God knew that their instructor had a loving heart and he would encourage them to deliver God's message to me. It was God's way of letting me know that not only does he listen to our prayers, he also answers them!

In my heart, I now know that my parents are happy and even though they are kept busy doing God's work and they are not available to be near me, they still love me and I am in their thoughts.

Oh, what a special and glorious 50th birthday I had! God's angels were sent to sing happy birthday to me!

I also know that I will never again hear my parent's voices singing happy birthday to me, but this experience will last a lifetime and I will always remember the sweet, angelic voices of God's angels. I will always believe that God answers our prayers!

Dear God,

Bless all the little children in the world. Let your angels from heaven watch over them, protect them and guide them thru life. Please keep them all safe and pure.

Touch each and every child and give them the assurance that Jesus and your angels are always with them.

Amen.

A CHILD'S MIND is so innocent and pure. It is uncluttered with the perplexing thoughts of everyday life. It's open to accepting new and wonderful things and absorbs hundreds of new sights and sounds each and every day. Every sight and sound is exciting and interesting. A child's perception of all it sees and hears has no flaws and it knows no right or wrong. Seeing, feeling, hearing and smelling something for the first time makes a clear and untainted impression. Their mind is like a clean slate just waiting to be etched upon. And because of this clear and unscarred mind, a child is capable to see things from a different perspective than an adult. This perspective is the most important difference between an adults mind and a child's mind. There are no previous thoughts that can challenge its views.

The ability to ACCEPT all it sees into an uncluttered mind without challenging or reasoning is only capable by a child. Their minds are always accepting new ideas without comparing previous knowledge. And it is capable of not intertwining thoughts with rationalization.

It is a child's "innocence and purity" that makes all children special to God. And God and his angel's have a special communication with children. I strongly believe that all little children are able to see God's angels – all the time. They see them everywhere. But, once they are old enough to realize who they are seeing, and are capable to describe them – they can no longer see their angels. Until, of course, when God decides that they are needed to be seen.

Its God's littlest of children that you will see giggle…..at nothing. Or they will smile at a blank wall. Or they can be sitting in their car seats, staring out the window and suddenly a smile comes across their face and they begin to laugh. What are they smiling at? What are they giggling at? What are they laughing at? Maybe it's an angel doing something funny. Or, maybe it's an angel whispering in their ear. Or, maybe it's an angel tickling their toes.

We'll never know. But I do believe that parents are not the only ones kissing their babies soft little cheeks as they lay them down to sleep!

# Danny's Angel

**"LOOK MOMMY!"** **"THERE'S AN ANGEL!"** Three year old Danny excitedly squealed as he pointed his little finger at the floor. Without a hesitating moment, Danny's mother spun her head around as she looked away from the computer screen. As she looked down, her eyes followed along the length of Danny's little outstretched arm to the tip of his tiny finger. She focused her eyes on the floor precisely to where her son was pointing. Out of the far corner of her eye, she could see that Danny's smile was stretched from ear to ear and his eyes were bursting with excitement. Simultaneously, his mother's eyes grew wide with amazement as her son's words began to register in her mind. With one quick blink she scanned the floor, looking in all directions. But she saw nothing. Nothing except her little son sitting with his legs crossed and a few toys scattered about. Instantly and with all of her heart, she wished that she too could see Danny's angel.

Unable to see anyone but Danny, she immediately asked him: "Where? - Where is the angel?" "RIGHT THERE!" he replied with the same enthusiasm as he had a moment ago. "IT'S RIGHT THERE!" he squealed again as his little arm continued to point to the floor with his chubby little forefinger extended. It was obvious that Danny was bubbling with excitement as his childlike, squeaky voice hit even a slightly higher pitch.

His mother, Casey, concentrated hard and looked down at the floor, but she still couldn't see the angel that her son was talking about. Her dark brown eyes grew even wider as she looked all around him. They glanced back and forth, scoping every inch of the floor, but still, she couldn't see the angel. Instead, she could see only the soft, white carpet on which her son Danny was sitting.

Disappointed and a little frustrated at not being able to see Danny's angel, Casey dropped her arms from the computer desk onto her lap. She turned slightly in her chair and thought for a quick moment. Without wasting a second, she decided to ask him more questions. She knew she had to act quickly. She wanted to know every tiny, little detail about Danny's angel and she didn't want to loose his attention. She also knew how quickly a child becomes distracted and she didn't want that to happen. Not this time!

Hundred's of questions flashed thru her mind and it was difficult for her to decide on which question to ask first. She wanted answers to them all. But, knowing she had to think fast, it took only a second for her to decide on what she thought would encourage Danny to describe what he was seeing. "Is it a big angel, honey?" she asked him. "NOOOO!" Danny answered with a much deeper, more serious tone in his voice. His long, thick eye lashes seemed to be holding his eyes wide open and without so much as a quick blink, they continued to twinkle with excitement. Casey could see that he was still as ecstatic as he was a moment ago. In fact, his whole body seemed to be exploding with happiness and excitement!

Casey, was still feeling her son's excitement, and knew that she had to think even faster. "Well, how big is it?" she questioned him again as she silently wished he would suddenly become very descriptive. It was evident that Danny really wanted his mommy to see his angel. He turned his head slightly and his big brown eyes looked up at his mother for only a split second. He smiled. He then turned his head and looked back to the floor where he was still pointing. "It's a LITTLE angel!" Danny answered as if to say: Silly mommy – Why are you asking? Don't you know? Can't you see the angel too? Danny turned his head again and looked at his mother. His facial expression changed. After a brief questioning look, his smile dropped and the look in his eyes clearly expressed the frustration that he was feeling.

The look on Danny's face changed once again. This time, he had a sad look of disappointment. He didn't understand why his mommy wasn't able to see his angel. Casey realized that he was confused and unable to grasp the idea that he was seeing something so clearly and prominent, but yet, his mother was acting like she wasn't able to confirm that she sees his angel too. Danny had quickly become very disappointed, and without saying another word, he got up from the floor from which he was sitting. He stood for only a second, and with not even so much as a glance towards his mother, he quickly ran off to play with his little brother in his toy filled bedroom. Danny left his mother sitting there with questions unanswered and a thousand thoughts flying thru her mind.

Casey sat staring at the floor while she tried to carefully organize the raging thoughts and wide spectrum of feelings that have begun to overtake her normally calm disposition. She was unable to move. Her arms were still resting on her lap. Her eyes were still focused on the floor where her son Danny had been sitting just seconds ago. She felt like she was in a state of shock and frozen amazement. She didn't want to move a muscle, in fear that it would change what had just happened. Only a few minutes had passed since her son Danny had demanded her attention with his announcement. A soft, pleasing smile slowly began to light up Casey's face. As she started to collect her thoughts, the excitement of what had just happened slowly began to overwhelm her. Her thoughts, one by one, fell into an orderly pattern and the reality of the past few minutes became clearer and clearer within her mind. Casey now realized that she had just witnessed the joy that her son was feeling as he saw one of God's heavenly creatures. A warm glow washed over Casey's entire body. It was a glow of pride and astonishment. She felt proud that her son wanted to share his vision with her. She could still feel his excitement as he told her about his angel. Oh, how she wished she could have seen Danny's angel too!

The computer softly hummed in the background and Casey sat perfectly still as her mind began to drift. She wondered what Danny's angel looked like…..

I can't help but think that Casey envisioned a small, chubby, childlike figure, about two years old in size, with a soft, creamy complexion and a sweet, innocent smile. Perhaps it had wispy, gentle curls of golden blonde, baby fine hair, just barely grazing its neck. Were its cheeks plump, with a delicate shadow of light pink? Did it have big, round, crystal clear blue eyes twinkling with the innocent beauty from within? Was it dressed in a cashmere soft, little white gown, trimmed in sparkling gold? Could this possibly be what Danny's little angel looked like? Or did it look completely different? Was it a child like figure, or perhaps it was an adult figure, only inches in size? Casey's thoughts envisioned what she thought Danny's angel looked like, but with no detailed description from Danny, Casey and I could only wonder if we were right or wrong. Danny, on the other hand, knows for sure.

Danny had been sitting on her newly laid, soft, white, carpeted floor, when he told his mother that he saw an angel. Was his angel sitting with its legs crossed? Was it a boy or a girl? Did Danny's little angel have wings? And, most importantly, where did the angel go? Did it follow Danny into his room or was the angel still sitting there, perhaps watching her? So many thoughts raced through her mind. Casey really wished she could have seen Danny's angel. She had so many questions that she wanted answers too. She couldn't help but wonder if she would ever find answers to her questions.

DANNY IS A three year old little boy with an intelligence level of a child much older than he really is. As all three year olds are, he is very inquisitive, but his thirst for knowledge is exceptional. His interest and comprehension of his environment and adult conversation is advanced far beyond his age. His mother, Casey, realized early on, that her son not only has the ability to learn adult conversation, but that he is also capable of understanding it and using it in his everyday life. She consistently encourages her son to learn and explore new words, thoughts and ideas. His vocabulary far exceeds the limits of a three year olds mind, and it's not unusual for him to use, but to also "understand" words such as: monochromatic or precipitation. Danny's memory is capable of storing information and details about everything he sees and hears, then recalling it almost instantly. He is persistent and expects logical and detailed answers to all his questions. Simple answers just are not good enough for him. He not only wants to know "why", but he also wants to hear every tiny detail regarding the subject of which he is learning and inquiring about.

Although Danny has a constant thirst to learn and absorb all that he sees and hears, he also understands that even at his young age, he should be very proud of himself. He seems to know that he is accomplishing things that a typical child his age, just doesn't do. After learning something new or experiencing something different, he proudly displays his accomplishments in his eyes and facial expressions. His happy child-like giggles and excited voice, combined with the sweetest smile, lets you see that he's ever so proud of himself. There is never any doubt that he doesn't realize he has learned something new. He projects enthusiasm for knowledge from every once of his little being!

Danny is 38 inches tall and weights only 37 pounds. He has short, course, light brown hair, a round little face with big brown eyes and the cutest, little pair of eye glasses! He has a smile that would melt any ones heart and his face glows with pride! At such a young age, his accomplishments are outstanding and he definitely does have a lot to be proud of!

# A Sense Of Humor

THE FOLLOWING DAY was Wednesday. Once a week, Casey and her two sons would spend the evening with their Grandma and Grandpa. It was during this one particular visit, that we had found out that angels have a sense of humor!

Gathered in the kitchen, at what seemed like a typical daily dinner, we were unaware of Casey's conversation intent. But we did however; notice her urgency to start a peaceful dinner. As she placed Danny in his highchair between herself and his grandpa, Danny took one look at the food on his tray and he began to protest – loudly. It was evident that he had expected his favorite food - macaroni and cheese - and not the roast beef and mashed potatoes that filled his dinner plate. With that one look at his plate, he quickly decided that before he would give in and eat his unwanted dinner, he would demand to have a Popsicle first. He had also decided that he wasn't about to settle for just any Popsicle. It had to be a yellow one. It was his choice of color for the day.

After watching displays of tantrums and stubbornness, Casey realized that giving in and letting him have his dessert first, would be a logical decision. She knew that once he devoured his Popsicle, he would then move on to eating his dinner in silence. And silence from the children, for the duration of dinner, was what she had wanted to accomplish. Casey had a lot on her mind and today's visit had a specific purpose for her. She could hardly wait to begin relating yesterday's experience to us and that thought alone prompted her to quickly give in to Danny's request.

Danny and his little brother sat in silence as they each began nibbling away at the banana flavored, yellow Popsicle's that he insisted upon them having. His face showed a look of accomplishment that proved he had won yet another battle within his childlike world. The accomplished smile on his face also showed that even at his young age, he knows that occasionally, it truly is possible to have your dessert and eat it too!

CASEY WAS STILL excited about the thoughts of yesterday, and it was obvious that she was anxious to tell us something. Her concentration wasn't centered on her children or on her dinner, but rather on the thoughts of how she would begin to tell us who her son had seen. Once Casey carefully gathered all of her thoughts together, she began to speak. Mechanically, mouthfuls of food slid down her throat unnoticed as she began to describe in complete detail what had occurred the day before.

She immediately caught our attention with her first sentence. As Casey spoke, I could feel her excitement and I silently wished that I too, had been there when Danny demanded her attention with his announcement. With each and every sentence, I envisioned not only what she was describing, but also what she must have felt like when she heard Danny's voice announcing his angel's presence. I couldn't help but anxiously wait to hear her next sentence.

The room fell silent for a short moment while Casey calmed her rapidly beating heart. She still had more to say and once again, she needed to collect her thoughts. She took a short breath to swallow a forkful of mashed potatoes, and then she glanced at Danny. It was obvious that he was oblivious to our conversation as he continued to run his little pink tongue over his hand, savoring every drop of his now dripping, banana Popsicle.

As Casey once again began to talk, a wave of goose bumps covered my entire body. The thought that OUR little grandson had seen an angel played over and over in my mind as I listened to her every word. By the time Casey had finished describing yesterday's event, we had all agreed that it's not common for a three year old to tell you that there's an angel sitting on the floor beside him!

Casey's description of yesterday definitely brought life to our typically dull dinner table conversation. Not only did she tell us about Danny's angel, she also was sharing with us the reality of one of God's heavenly secrets. And knowing this, she was unable to hide any excitement within her existence. As she spoke, her voice projected astonishment with each sentence. Her eyes twinkled and her face seemed to have a radiant glow. She looked as if she had just swallowed a ray of sunshine and it was lighting up her entire being!

Both her father and I felt proud, that our grandson was knowledgeable enough to understand that seeing an angel is a very special honored event. The fact that he was excited enough to call his mothers attention to his angel, made us realize that he too understood the uniqueness of his vision. We had even realized how honored we felt that God allowed us to hear first hand, directly from Casey, about Danny's angel.

DANNY OF COURSE, was still in "Popsicle" heaven. Three tiny pieces had fallen onto his tray from the now empty stick, and he leaned forward to suck up each and every melting piece with his tiny puckered lips. After slurping up the last of the three remaining pieces, Danny lifted his head and his now sticky face smiled with contentment. He had shown us that he was still the boss of the dinner table!

Once again, he was very proud of himself and his accomplishment and he now felt content enough to move on to eating from his dinner plate, the little chunks of roast beef and the now cold mashed potatoes.

Still in awe, we began to ask Casey for more information. We had the same questions running through our minds as she had the day before. We wanted to know all the details, just as she had wanted to know. But unfortunately, she couldn't give us any more information than she already had told us, and our discussion left questions unanswered. We all felt that the answers to our questions would always remain a mystery.

As our topic of conversation continued on, Danny remained eating his dinner in silence. He didn't show any signs of listening to our conversation as he still seemed to be deep in "Popsicle thought". That is when we discovered that "Danny" may have not been listening to our conversation, but apparently his angel was!

The more we talked, the more our conversation led to a specific topic: DO ANGELS HAVE WINGS? It was within minutes that we received an answer to our question, but it definitely wasn't what we had expected. We did not find out if all angels have wings. We did however; discover that angels DO have a sense of humor!

CAPTURING DANNY'S ATTENTION was now easy for his grandpa to do, since the Popsicle was now non-existent. Leaning forward and looking directly into Danny's eyes, he asked him if he remembered seeing the angel yesterday. Danny quickly replied with a smile and a "Yes". Now, confident that he had Danny's full attention and that he was making progress, his grandpa decided to ask him the question that was burning on all of our minds. While still staring directly into Danny's big brown eyes, he blurted out the question and asked him: "Danny, did the angel have wings?" Danny continued to show interest in the subject as his thin, light brown eye brows rose slightly and turned inward. A quick look of inward thinking washed over his face. He was concentrating on the question that his grandpa had just asked him. The room seemed to get very quiet. No one said a word. It was as if we were all frozen in time – anxiously waiting for Danny's answer. Even Danny sat perfectly still. Then, slowly, the look of deep thought faded from his face and his little head cocked slightly to his right side. We could see that Danny's thoughts seemed to be distracted and he had stopped thinking about the question. His eyes were no longer focused on his grandpa – or anyone else. They had a distant look and his attention was clearly directed at something other than us. He remained very still and silent. Danny acted like he was "listening" to something. But, what was he listening too? We weren't talking. We were all silent. Even his little brother wasn't making a sound. All our eyes were focused on Danny as we sat staring at him, anxiously awaiting his answer. We could see that he was definitely listening and hearing something, but, we didn't know what. Was someone talking to him? WHO could possibly be talking to him? It wasn't us.

A few quick moments of silence had pasted. Then suddenly, Danny smiled. Then he giggled. One little giggle. It was a soft, cute little giggle. Then his eyes twinkled and he let out another giggle. It was almost as if someone was tickling him. Then he went silent. No more giggles. Instantly, Danny lifted his head up high and straightened his back as his chubby little hands reached out and grabbed a hold of the far edges of his highchair tray. His upper body leaned forward as far as it could and his whole sticky little face brightened with a smile. It was a big, bright, inner silliness smile. Danny's big brown eyes were now, once again, focused on his grandpa. Their eyes locked. Danny's smile turned into a proud grin as he blurted out in a loud demanding voice: "CHICKENS HAVE WINGS!"

Danny's words took only seconds to register in our stunned and shocked minds. Meanwhile, Danny's facial expression changed. The smile disappeared from his face. He looked scared and confused at our silence and shocked expressions. He wasn't sure if he had said something bad or good. He began to look worried. His hands released the sides of his highchair tray and his little body sunk back into his chair. His puzzled eyes moved back and forth to each of us, contemplating what would happen next. He was worried about the consequences of what he had just said to his grandpa.

A moment later, the shock of Danny's reply began to wear off and we all simultaneously burst into laughter. Danny's confused look slowly faded away and he began to laugh with us. At first he seemed to be a little hesitant, but his laugher quickly matched ours. We could literally see a sense of relief wash over him as he realized that what he had said was not something bad. He also realized that we thought what he had said was funny - even if he himself didn't understand why. Danny was once again happy. A proud smile now displayed across his face. He had done well. Danny was pleased with Danny. He could once again be proud of himself!

To us, it was quite obvious that Danny didn't understand the "meaning" of his short sentence. Once the words left his lips, and he saw our silent, shocked faces, for those few short moments, Danny was scared. He was scared of the repercussion of his comment. At that very moment, we could see that Danny honestly didn't have a clue as to "why" we were laughing. He was really confused. It wasn't until our laughter began, that Danny realized that he must have said something that we had obviously thought was funny. Our laughter gave Danny approval to laugh too.

For a few moments after our laughter had ceased, we sat in silence as the reality and belief of what we had just heard register within our minds. We then couldn't help but laugh once again at Danny's innocent response to the question that he was asked. Although, it was difficult to believe what we had just heard him say, we realized that the answer to his Grandpa's question was merely only "presented" by Danny. We highly doubted that a three year old had the ability to make a comparison between angels, chickens and wings. A child that young can repeat a joke that they have heard, but the ability to invent one, just isn't in their realm of capabilities – no matter how intelligent they are. We do know however, that Danny's angel was listening to our conversation and that it was his angel that whispered in his ear the answer to his grandpa's question. Danny only repeated what he had heard and was told to say.

We now know that angels definitely DO have a sense of humor. But we still do not know if Danny's angel had wings. Danny knows – but he's not telling.

Is he not supposed to tell? I believe that when Danny was asked the question - which he definitely would have answered – his angel distracted him before he got a chance to tell us. God has his reasons for us not to know what Danny's angel looked like, and because of that, we decided not to question Danny any further.

God's angels are all around us. They are our guardians and they watch over us. They are our connection to heaven. They deliver messages to us from God. They never leave us and they are there when we need them most. All we need to do is ask them for help and they help us. God's angels will always be a mystery to us and I believe God wants to keep it that way. God has his way of showing us glimpses of his heavenly creatures, not only to intrigue us, but to strengthen our faith in him. Like his angel's, God is always watching over us and he knows precisely the exact moment we need him or his angels.

MANY OF US have a philosophy that we live by. Some of us even have several philosophies that we try to incorporate into our every day lives. I'm one of those people who have more than one philosophy. Actually, there are two of them that I believe in and they are both very simple.

The first one is: Everything happens for a reason. The second one is: Everything always works out the way it's supposed too.

Over the years, these two philosophy's have become a strong base for me and they have helped me accept and cope, on a daily basis, with many pleasant and some unpleasant events in my life. But recently, I have chosen to replace my number one philosophy with a very important bible verse that has come to mean a lot to me. I have placed this bible verse high above any philosophy or any other words of wisdom.

# A Bible Verse To Live By

BY NATURE, I am a slightly hyper person and I tend to keep myself extremely active. I always try to look on the positive side of life and feel that that outlook has helped me to survive the many small and large trials and tribulations of every day life. Anyone who personally knows me will admit that it's almost as if I strive on excitement and the little bumps of turbulence that come my way. Life for me has never been dull and I have learned to accept that and embrace each new day, no matter what it brings my way. In fact, I have a special little magnet that has become a daily reminder to me that my life just isn't supposed to be boring!

Many years ago, my husband bought me a refrigerator magnet while he was away on a business trip. It has come to mean a lot to me and I will always treasure it. The little magnet is approximately two and half inches by two and half inches square. It has a copper colored frame with a piece of glass covering the picture underneath it. The little frame holds a picture of a beach landscape with the ocean stretching out to a small, tree covered island. In the foreground, a little row boat is centered in the middle of the beach, resting between a little mound of sand and a large clump of beach grass. It's a pretty picture that suggests a very peaceful and calming atmosphere. Above the picture, in bold black type are the words: I can't relax. Tension is what's holding me together!"

Now, just looking at that magnet, one wouldn't think that there would be a whole lot of specialness to it, but for me – there is. You see, one day, shortly after I received the magnet, I accidently bumped it off of the refrigerator door and it fell crashing down to the floor. It shattered the little piece of glass that covered the calming picture, but the glass itself did not fall out. It remained shattered within the frame. I had felt really bad about breaking the magnet that my husband gave me, but one day, my very wise daughter put the whole incident into perspective. She said that the broken glass inside the frame now added more character to the magnet and that characteristic only intensified the meaning behind the words. You see, it's the tension from the frame that is holding the glass in place and it's the tension in my life that also holds me together! So I guess you could say that I'm similar to a shattered piece of glass that won't fall apart because no matter what happens, God is the shiny frame in my life that holds me together!

SATURDAY MORNING TRAFFIC was light and I had time to spare before my luncheon meeting at a near by restaurant. A friend and I were taking on new positions as chairmen in one of the wide variety of support groups that were hosted by the expanding medical facility in our county.

The road that I was traveling on was all too familiar to me and I barely had to concentrate on which direction I was headed. I was anxious to attend this meeting and looked forward to the wealth of information I was about to receive from the exiting chairman. She is a very knowledgeable lady and she was willing to share her treasure chest of information with us. I was excited to be embarking on a new adventure!

At the bottom of the long hill, I could see the bright yellow caution light that hung over the four way intersection. I had mentally calculated that the light would turn red by the time I reached the bottom of the hill and I mechanically started applying the brakes of my car, coming to a complete stop just before the cross walk stripes in the road. I was first in line in the turning lane to turn left onto the crossing road.

As I sat behind the wheel of my little sports car at the stop light, I glanced around as a larger vehicle pulled up along side of me. A few cars came to a stop behind me in the left turning lane and I was aware of their presence behind me. I applied my left turn signal and sat patiently waiting for the light to turn green and give me an arrow to proceed into the left turn.

My thoughts were random and seemed to flutter around, until they momentarily stopped as I remembered something important that I had forgotten to do. It was actually a little ritual of mine that I have done for many, many years. Out of pure habit from my Catholic upbringing, upon starting my car, I would use my right hand to make the sign of the cross and say a little prayer asking Jesus to protect me and bring me to and from my destination safely. Today, amid my anticipation about attending the meeting, I had forgotten to say my little prayer. Upon remembering this, I mentally began to say my little prayer and automatically my right hand went up to my forehead to begin to make the sign of the cross. As I did this, my head turned swiftly to the right. I could see the large vehicle sitting beside me and its driver was looking down at my shiny red car. My eyes quickly darted to my rear view mirror and from there I could see each of the three cars waiting patiently behind me for the light to change and give us a green arrow. From my position, I knew that the people inside all of the surrounding vehicles would be able to see what I was doing. I hesitated for only a second before I decided to continue to finish my ritual, all along knowing that the people surrounding me might be watching me. I finished my prayer and as a smile lifted the edges of my lips upward, I heard my mind recite a simple bible verse.

Matthew 10:33

"But whoever denies Me before men, him I will also deny before My Father who is in heaven.

That one little verse from the bible completely expressed my current thoughts and feelings. It also enabled me to realize that I truly wasn't ashamed to have anyone witness that I had just said a prayer. I admitted to myself that I believe in prayer and I wasn't embarrassed to show that I do. Of course, I didn't know for absolute sure if any of the people in the vehicles beside or behind me saw the gesture that I had just made. But, I was soon convinced that whether or not the present motorist had seen me, someone far more important had seen my gesture and heard my thoughts. A moment later I was thoroughly convinced that the little gesture that I made, most likely had just saved my life!

Out of the corner of my left eye I could see an expensive, silver SUV attempting to make a right hand turn as he sped around the corner. Spontaneously, both of my eyes focused on the front of the vehicle. I could visually see that it was traveling at a speed that was much too fast to safely maneuver a vehicle of that size thru a right hand turn. The fast speeding SUV was aimed directly at me! The vehicle wasn't attempting to slow down and my driver's side car door – beside which I was sitting – was its target. The only reaction that I had time for was to scream. The impulsive, blood curdling scream destroyed my smile as it made its escape from deep within my throat. My eye lids quickly squeezed shut in fear of watching the SUV crashing directly into me. There just wasn't time for me to react or do much of anything else. Within a second later, I heard the sound of a loud thud and crunching metal, with the aftermath of shattering glass and the high pitched tinkle of its small fragments hitting the pavement.

I then listened to the ear piercing sound of screeching brakes as the SUV came to a stop along the curb on the opposite side of the road.

In the silence that immediately followed the sound of screeching brakes, my brain analyzed the sequences of the different sounds that I had just heard. It had quickly told me that the previous sounds came from a slight distance behind me. They had not reverberated directly from my vehicle. My eye lids quickly flew open as I surrendered to the impulse to look and to verify to myself that I was correct in assessing that there wasn't any damage to my car. My nerves were definitely shook up, but I was greatly relieved to see that my car and I had escaped harm. The driver in the SUV realized that he had lost control over his vehicle, and in a panic, he must have jerked the steering wheel. Fortunately for me, the angle of his SUV was suddenly changed. He momentarily collided with the front end of the car sitting directly behind me. That inexperienced young driver didn't cause physical harm to anyone, but he did do extensive damage both his vehicle and the vehicle behind me.

The driver of the SUV had later explained that he had attempted to take the corner at too fast of a speed and the cup of water that had been balancing on the console between him and his younger sister had tipped over. The liquid drenched his gray flannel shorts which in turn, drew his attention away from concentrating on his driving. The sudden wet feeling shocked him and caused him to momentarily divert his eyes from the road as he glanced down at his wet shorts – all the while, keeping his foot on the accelerator. When he brought his eyes back to the road, he saw that his vehicle was aimed directly at me with only my car door separating me from the front grill of his SUV.

I can't help but to think that God's angels were there to protect me that morning. I believe that they alerted the young driver and brought back his awareness of the situation – just in the nick of time. I also can't help but to think of what could have happened had I been too ashamed to show that I pray and that I believe in the power of prayer. I know that God's angels are always beside us and they witnessed that I wasn't afraid or ashamed to display my belief in God and Jesus above, so in turn, I believe that they helped me knowing that God himself would not deny me because I was not afraid or embarrassed to acknowledge him.

JUST PREVIOUSLY, THE week before, I had encountered another very undeniable experience that made me realize that it wasn't "just a coincidence or an act of luck", but it was indeed an act of God and his angels. The past week held another small test of faith for me and this particular test proved yet once more, that at any moment in time, we can be called upon to prove our faith.

Now, if you've ever been in southern California, you've probably encountered an unforgettable ride on the famous 91 freeway. It's definitely something that not only Californian's constantly remark or complain about, but its one of the most memorable things that visitors to this sunshiny area will talk about upon their return to their home state. The 91 freeway makes a lasting impression on anyone who has had the experience to drive on one of southern California's most famous freeways.

For the most part, the 91 freeway is four lanes across, which often expands anywhere from five to seven lanes to allow vehicles to make their entrance or exit. There is a car pool lane and / or a toll lane that runs along the left side of the freeway. In sections of the 91 freeway, the car pool / toll lanes consist of two lanes that are separated from the regular traffic with plastic sticks that are attached onto the roadway. Those sticks act as a barrier that creates the car pool / toll road lanes. Either exiting from or entering into the toll lanes is only allowed at specific designated points along the freeway. Add to this a very thick congestion of hundreds of cars, all going at or above the allowed speed limit while they are anxiously trying to reach their destinations and you will get a very tense drive. Most drivers who commute on the 91 freeway will admit that they are in a constant fear that traffic will back up and they will be caught sitting in a freeway gridlock without any chance of escaping. These traffic backups have been known to bring out the nastiness in people and no one is immune from some degree of road rage when they realize that are trapped in the middle of a freeway parking lot and that they will now be late at arriving to their designated destination.

Driving on the 91 freeway in California has often been compared to driving on a race track. The anxiety that begins to mount inside you as you drive onto the entrance ramp is exhilarating and yet stressful at the same time. Hardly anyone stays in one lane and if you had the ability to look down at the freeway from above, you would think that it was a cut throat race to the finish! Although, there is a good aspect of the 91 freeway that I feel I should point out to you, and that is: upon reaching your exit, you release a huge sigh of relief and that can literally help to aid in clearing your lungs for better breathing!

I happen to have a real love for driving and unlike others; I don't mind driving on the 91 freeway.

Once again I was behind the wheel of my car as I drove up the ramp to enter onto the 91 freeway. I was headed to my daughter's house to babysit for my grandchildren. It was late afternoon on Friday and rush hour traffic spanned across every lane. Cars and trucks of all makes and models were speeding along as usual and refusing to allow anyone to get in front of them. It was obvious that they all had one mission in mind, and that was to arrive at their destination as quickly as they possibly could after a long day at work.

Perched at the top of the entrance ramp was a little red and green flashing stop and go light which helps to regulate the merging traffic onto the freeway. Each vehicle must wait his turn to enter the speedway race. I anxiously awaited my turn as I surveyed all the swift moving vehicles speeding past me on my left. I was pleased to see a tiny, little break in traffic which gave me a clearing to enter the freeway when the light turned green.

I safely made it across two lanes! Now I had only three more lanes to maneuver across before I would encounter the plastic poles that would prohibit me from entering the toll lanes. My head swiveled around quickly as I glanced beside me, in front of me and into my rear view mirror. Seeing that the clearing on my left side was still available, I felt it was safe to move over into the next lane.

I am very good at multi-tasking and although I had earlier performed my little ritual upon entering my car, I didn't resist the urge to repeat my ritual once again. I quickly asked Jesus for extra protection.

The lane beside me had a break in traffic, which would allow me to move one lane closer to my destination. I took a second swift glance to be sure that no other vehicle was approaching in the lane beside me. The lane was still empty. As my car began to just barely cross over the white dotted lines, out of what seemed like nowhere, a large silver pick up truck appeared right beside my car door! Apparently, he had decided that he would cross over two lanes of traffic in an effort be in front of me in my lane.

If I could have jumped out of my skin, I am sure that is exactly what I would have done! For a startling moment, he was traveling at the same speed that I was maintaining and his vehicle was getting closer and closer to me. It was so close beside me that I could have literally touched his side door without the effort of extending my arm at full length!

Oddly enough, I remained very calm and a peaceful feeling gracefully washed over me. I felt a very special blessing at that moment. I felt surrounded and protected.

I couldn't actually see it, but I felt that there was a thick invisible barrier wedged between the pick up truck next to me and my car. It was like an invisible bumper made of air that was protecting my car from becoming a projectile missile that would have been launched sideways.

The silver truck quickly sped off ahead of me and continued to move over into my lane. I was amazed to see that the lanes beside me remained completely clear of traffic all the way into the toll lane!

I honestly had felt as if all the other surrounding vehicles had moved and were cleared out of my way. I was then able to safely proceed across two more lanes to enter into the toll lane.

For the rest of my twenty minute journey to my daughter's house, I was able to play the scenario over and over again in my minds eye, while I repeatedly thanked Jesus for answering my prayer. His sent his angels to protect me and they fulfilled my prayer request.

Angels are the creation of God. They are a blessing from God to us. God uses his angels to communicate, protect and minister to us.

God reaches his hand to you through the works of his angels. They are continuously beside us as we walk thru life. And God himself is the infinite source that supplies us with the support, strength and courage that we need to face even the teeniest stresses in life. This infinite source is always readily available to each and every one of us and it can easily be obtained by anyone thru the act of prayer.

But always remember to be thankful! Each day of our lives is truly a precious gift from God and we need to thank him often for the time and all the blessings that we have been given. We never know when our time is up or when we will be put to a test to prove our devotion and faith in God above. We need to always be ready so that we are not caught off guard and we should always be prepared for the challenge!

Above Us, Below Us.
Before Us, Behind Us.
Beside Us.
In every imaginable place,
An Angel is with you!

# The Lords Prayer
## Matthew 6:9

Our Father in heaven,
Hallowed be Your name.
Your kingdom come.
Your will be done
On earth as it is in heaven.
Give us this day our daily bread.
And forgive us our debts,
As we forgive our debtors.
But deliver us from the evil one.
For Yours is the kingdom and the power and
The glory forever.  Amen.

# About the author:

BORN AND RAISED in Bedford, Ohio, Sandra always had a passion for writing. She has volunteered for many editorial positions in various organizations and clubs throughout her life. She is actively involved in a local support group for Trigeminal Neuralgia and believes that each person can make a difference in all of the lives that they touch.

Sandra now resides in Southern California with her husband Timothy and she spends most of her spare time with her two children and four grandchildren. She treasures each moment spent with her family and captures it all into memory by constantly taking photos with her cameras. Aside from her family, her favorite hobbies are cooking, photography and crafts.

It wasn't until after her second grandson was born, that she was inspired to write and share her experiences with the world. In this book, she tells us of several significant events that have affected her life with a powerful impact. She looks forward to collecting information and inspirational events to include them in her future publishing's.

Sandra is also currently working with her grandson on writing a series of unique books about Autism. Together they hope to further open the window into the lives of families living with autistic children.